Anger Management for Parents with Kids 3-7

Easy DBT Workbook to Develop Coping Skills, Achieve Instant Emotional Regulation, and Master Peaceful Parenting to Raise Resilient Children

By SpreadLife Publishing

Copyright © 2024 by SpreadLife Publishing

All rights reserved.

It is not legal to reproduce, duplicate, or transmit any part of this document in either electronic means or printed format. Recording of this publication is strictly prohibited and any storage of this document is not allowed unless with written permission from the publisher, except for the use of brief quotations in a book review.

The content contained within this book may not be reproduced, duplicated, or transmitted without direct written permission from the author or the publisher.

Under no circumstances will any blame or legal responsibility be held against the publisher or author for any damages, reparation, or monetary loss due to the information contained within this book, either directly or indirectly. You are responsible for your own choices, actions, and results.

Legal Notice:

This book is copyright protected. This book is only for personal use. You cannot amend, distribute, sell, use, quote, or paraphrase any part or the content within this book without the consent of the author or publisher.

Disclaimer Notice:

Please note the information contained within this document is for educational and entertainment purposes only. All effort has been executed to present accurate, up-to-date, reliable, and complete information. No warranties of any kind are declared or implied. Readers acknowledge that the author is not rendering legal, financial, medical, or professional advice. The content within this book has been derived from various sources. Please consult a licensed professional before attempting any techniques outlined in this book.

By reading this document, the reader agrees that under no circumstances is the author responsible for any losses, direct or indirect, which are incurred as a result of the use of the information contained within this document, including, but not limited to, errors, omissions, or inaccuracies.

Contents

Introduction 1
Part One: Foundations of Emotional Regulation 4
   Chapter One: Understanding Emotional Regulation 5
      Exploring the Impact of Unregulated Emotions on Parenting 6
      The Impact of Culture and Family on Emotional Regulation 11
      Common Challenges to Emotional Regulation in Children 13
      The Basics of Dialectical Behavior Therapy (DBT) for Parents 16
      The Science of Emotions: A Parent's Guide 19
      Building Emotional Awareness: Mindfulness Techniques 20
      Identifying Triggers and Emotional Responses 22
      Embracing Emotions: Validation and Acceptance 23
      Practical Worksheet: My Emotional Journal 25
      Takeaway One 29
   Chapter Two: Mastering Anger Management 31
      Understanding the Physiology of Anger 32
      The Psychology of Anger 36
      The Angry Parent Trap: Common Triggers 40
      DBT Skills for Anger: Distress Tolerance 42
      Cognitive Restructuring for Parental Anger 44
      Communication Strategies to Prevent Explosions 46
      Teaching Your Child Healthy Anger Management 48
      Guided Visualization for Anger Release 49
      Practical Worksheet: My Anger Control Plan 50
      Takeaway Two 54
Part Two: Parenting with DBT and Coping Skills 55
   Chapter Three: Anxiety Coping Skills for Parents 56
      Recognizing Anxiety Patterns in Parenting 58
      Mindful Breathing and Relaxation Techniques 60
      Grounding Exercises for Anxiety 62

- Building Resilience: Emotional Regulation in Stressful Situations.... 66
- Developing a Daily Calming Routine 67
- Practical Worksheet: My Anxiety Coping Toolbox 70
- Takeaway Three 74

Chapter Four: Anxiety Coping Skills for Kids (Ages 3-7) 75
- Understanding Childhood Anxiety 76
- Child-Friendly Mindfulness Practices 84
- Creative Expression for Anxiety Relief 86
- The Power of Play: Games to Manage Anxiety................................. 87
- Gradual Exposure Techniques for Kids 93
- Practical Worksheet: My Child's Anxiety Coping Plan 99
- Takeaway Four 101

Chapter Five: Modeling Emotional Regulation 104
- Understanding Emotional Regulation in Kids Aged 3-7 105
- Why Kids Learn from Parents' Emotions.. 109
- Practicing Emotion Regulation Together 113
- Empathy and Validation in Parenting.. 117
- Teaching Children to Express Their Emotions 121
- Role-Playing to Improve Parent-Child Interactions 123
- Practical Worksheet: Our Emotion Regulation Action Plan........... 126
- Takeaway Five 132

Part Three: Building a Happy and Resilient Family 134
Chapter Six: Overcoming Perfectionism 136
- The Perfectionist Parenting Dilemma 137
- DBT Techniques for Letting Go of Perfection................................ 141
- Building Self-Confidence as a Parent 143
- Setting Realistic Expectations for Yourself and Your Child 146
- Embracing Mistakes as Learning Opportunities.............................. 151
- Coping With Parenting Challenges.. 153
- Nurturing Confidence Resilience in Your Child 157
- Takeaway Six... 163

Chapter Seven: Strengthening the Parent-Child Bond 165

    Building Trust and Connection 166
    Cultivating Empathy in Parenting 169
    Effective Listening and Validation 172
    Conflict Resolution Strategies 175
    Quality Time: Meaningful Activities with Kids 180
    Reinforcing Positive Behaviors 183
    Practical Worksheet: Our Bond-Building Playbook 184
    Takeaway Seven 187
Chapter Eight: Embracing a Peaceful, Happy Life 188
    Reflecting on Your Parenting Journey 190
    Celebrating Progress and Successes 193
    Maintaining Consistency in DBT Skills 195
    Self-Care for Lasting Peace and Happiness 197
    Balancing Work and Family Life 199
    Building a Support System 202
    Practical Worksheet: My Ongoing Peace and Happiness Plan 206
    Takeaway Eight 211

Conclusion 214
References 218

Introduction

"My biggest parenting conundrum: Why is it so hard to put someone who is already sleepy to sleep."

–Chrissy Teigen

Being a parent has never been easy. Don't get me wrong, I have experienced the joy and sheer delight it brings. Having my little girl squeeze my pinky while she is suckling and calling me "Dada" when she is old enough are moments that fill my heart with warmth and love. However, parenting also comes with its fair share of challenges. The sleepless nights, the worries that keep you awake, and the constant juggling between work, household chores, and caring for your child can sometimes be overwhelming.

As they grow older, you get to deal with spiraling emotions. One moment, they are sweet and lovey-dovey; the next, they are sassy and getting you worked up. Now, you have to learn how to train your kids to be well-behaved while being on your best behavior at all times, and I agree with you; that's not easy, not one bit.

Parenting is a complex, skill-based task that involves regulating several daily emotions. According to data published in the Journal of Marriage and Family, 74% of parents acknowledged yelling or screaming at their kids, with 1 in 4 saying they cursed or used swear words. It gets worse: In a nationally representative survey (Straus & Field 2003), approximately 90% of American parents reported one or more instances of harsh verbal discipline toward children of all ages. As expected, this does not yield good results for the kids. A study from the National Institutes of Health found a direct correlation between children's aggressive behavior and frequent yelling from their mothers. Firm verbal reprimand from parents causes social and behavioral issues in adolescents.

In the pages ahead, we'll learn several DBT (Dialectical Behavior Therapy) techniques to help you manage anger and anxiety effectively, teaching you how to model emotional regulation for your children. This book will provide tools to manage anxiety and introduce strategies that encourage gradual exposure for you and your kids, creating a more relaxed and confident parenting style. You will also learn to acknowledge imperfections and adapt to the dynamic nature of parenting, resulting in a more open and understanding relationship with your children.

I am a parent who loves to help other parents overcome issues with their emotional struggles, particularly those surrounding parenting challenges. You can be sure what I am about to offer valuable advice because I know what I am talking about: I have been studying the best methods for emotional regulation and avoiding negative patterns for more than five years now.

Helping you achieve freedom from emotional struggles matters deeply to me because what you are about to learn helped me overcome these issues and become more confident in parenting. I understand how difficult it might seem to handle your emotions while parenting, and, as such, I can show you how to work things out without stress. I am confident that the strategies I share with you will help you immensely, having had plenty of practical experience.

I'm happy to have you join me on this journey. I hope the experiences and lessons I share in the pages ahead will bless you as much as they have blessed me. Don't give up on yourself just yet. You can be the parent you have always longed to be.

I'm rooting for you!

PART ONE
Foundations of Emotional Regulation

The truth is that there is no perfect way to think or feel. You are entitled to your feelings and emotions, but it's important to learn how to control and manage them, especially for the sake of your kids.

You can learn to control how you express your emotions even if you can't control how you feel. Negative emotions can be helpful. For example, pain and fear trigger adrenaline, the fight-or-flight hormone. This signals your brain and helps you think fast and act quickly if you're in danger.

All emotions are helpful and have something to teach you. You should learn to acknowledge and express your emotions healthily. Bottling up your emotions can lead to problems.

The first part of this book is dedicated to emotional regulation, and in the following two chapters, you will learn how to build emotional awareness. I will also show you some proven strategies to defuse anger and communicate effectively.

Let's dive in!

CHAPTER ONE

Understanding Emotional Regulation

Post this at all the intersections, dear friends: Lead with your ears, follow up with your tongue, and let anger straggle along in the rear.

— James 1:19-21 (MSG)

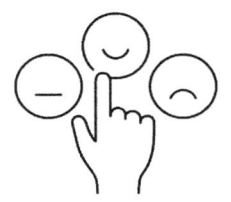

I once heard the story of a little boy whose fingers were broken by his father. They planned to fix a car together, and things started nice. The father showed the boy how to use tools and carve letters onto the wooden table in the workshop. The little boy got pretty excited and decided to put his newfound knowledge to use. He wanted to surprise his dad, so he scratched, "I love you, Dad," into the car's shiny paint. His heart was in the right place, but his choice was not.

The father was enraged when he saw the scratches. He'd just finished paying off the car, and just some days ago, he'd gotten a fresh coat of paint. I'm sure I'd be very upset, too. In his rage, he got a hold of the little boy, and things quickly got out of hand. By the time his rage subsided, his son's fingers were broken. Upon interrogation, he explained that in trying to correct the child (or vent his anger), he placed the nail between the boy's fingers and squeezed hard. He did not stop until he heard cracks.

Sad, right? There are several other stories of how their parents physically injured their kids simply because the father or mother did not learn to control their anger. Beyond physical deformities, many other kids and adolescents suffer from various kinds of trauma and mental-related issues due to verbal and psychological abuse from their parents. Your fear, anxiety, and negative emotions can take a great toll on your kids if you do not learn to regulate your emotions.

Emotional regulation is managing your emotions and how you react to them. Emotions are a normal part of the human experience. We experience various emotions daily, from joy when we take a surprise trip to frustration when we arrive late for an occasion. Depending on many factors, these feelings might range in intensity from severe to mild. Someone else might become outraged over an occurrence that barely fazes you, and vice versa. This spectrum of emotions can sometimes be hard to predict and even harder to control, which is why emotional regulation is necessary.

Exploring the Impact of Unregulated Emotions on Parenting

Case Study

Emily hissed as she switched off her alarm. Another day, another drama, she thought as she stood up to get her three young kids ready for school.

"Mommy, I can't find Dumbo!" Jason cried out, his voice echoing through the hallway.

Her heart raced when she heard this. She'd told Jason to put his toys away, but he never listened. He wound up looking for one of his toys every other day.

Her second child, Emma, refused to eat her cereal. "Mommy, I want pancakes," she whined, tears welling in her eyes.

Emily felt her frustration bubbling up. She made sure to set aside time in her hectic mornings to provide her children with breakfast, only for Emma to reject it for the third time this week. She wanted to shake some sense into Emma, but what would that solve?

She was still struggling to keep her emotions in check when Evan, her youngest, spilled his juice all over the kitchen floor.

Her patience reached a breaking point. She clenched her fists, her breath coming in short, ragged gasps.

You've probably been in Emily's shoes. You've been dealing with constant demands and endless tantrums, and one day, you just can't take it anymore.

According to the American Society for the Positive Care of Children, 14% of all men and 36% of women in prison in the USA were abused as children, about twice the frequency seen in the general population. Not being able to regulate your emotions can have short- and long-term effects on your children.

Emotional dysregulation can make it difficult to respond effectively and adequately to your child's needs. Imagine having to deal with a request from your son to play soccer when all you want to do is cry because you're already struggling with a pile of unpaid bills.

Emotional struggles can run in families. Studies have shown that if you don't learn how to manage your emotions from your parents, you might pass on these challenges to your children, even if you don't mean to (Yehuda *et al.* 2015).

This is because emotions can be deeply rooted in our past. When parents experience trauma or other difficult emotions, they might have trouble regulating them. This can make it difficult to teach their children how to regulate theirs.

Your child observes how you handle stress, anger, and sadness. They learn from your example. So, if you struggle to regulate your emotions, there is a higher chance they will face similar difficulties as they grow up. So, you have to break this cycle for their sake and yours.

Your child's emotional well-being is closely tied to the quality of your relationship. When your emotions are all over the place, it can affect the attachment between you and your child. Your inconsistent emotional responses might make them feel uncertain and anxious about your love and support.

A secure parent-child attachment gives a safe emotional base for your child to explore the world. But if your emotions are consistently hippity-hoppity, it can disrupt this secure attachment, creating potential problems in your relationship as they get older.

Disciplining kids is important, but it can be hard when feeling overwhelmed. When you are angry or frustrated, you might discipline them differently or too harshly. This can confuse and scare kids because they don't know what to expect. They might not understand why they're punished more severely for some things than others. This can hurt their development, making it harder for them to learn from their mistakes and take responsibility.

If you co-parent, emotional dysregulation can be even harder to deal with. It can be stressful for your child when you and your co-parent fight. Seeing you two argue can upset them and hurt their emotional health.

Emotional dysregulation can make it difficult to communicate effectively with your co-parent, especially when you are overwhelmed by your emotions. Some situations make it hard to stay calm and collected, even if you're trying. Emotional dysregulation can also make it difficult to agree on parenting decisions. You and your co-parent might have different parenting styles and values, which can be exacerbated when you struggle to manage your emotions.

Without emotional intelligence, you are more likely to react inappropriately to your children's feelings, which can cause stress and conflict. You might also have a more challenging time teaching your kids how to control their emotions. On the other hand, when you have emotional intelligence, you are better equipped to comprehend and control your emotions.

To make it worse, children might experience feelings of insecurity and anxiety, which can make it more difficult for them to develop the ability to control their emotions. This is because they might feel like they are not in control of their emotions and worry about what others will think of them.

Children who feel anxious can be more likely to worry about things out of their control, making it difficult to focus and concentrate. They can also have difficulty trusting others, making it difficult for them to learn how to cope with difficult emotions in a healthy way.

Unregulated emotions can also significantly impact your children's development and well-being. Children struggling to regulate their emotions can have problems making and keeping friends. They are also prone to anger, lashing out, or withdrawing from social situations, which can lead to isolation and loneliness. These kids can also struggle to pay attention in class, follow instructions, and complete assignments. They might also be more likely to get into trouble at school.

It doesn't end there: The inability to regulate your emotions can also increase your risk of developing mental health problems such as anxiety, depression, and behavioral issues. Struggling to manage your emotions also makes you more susceptible to unhealthy coping mechanisms like substance abuse. This can further impair your parenting abilities and foster a stressful environment for your children.

If you find yourself relying on substances to cope with emotions, get help, and get it fast. Your child's future depends on your ability to address these issues: The impact of unregulated emotions on your child is not limited to their childhood years. These effects can stretch into adulthood, affecting their relationships, mental health, and overall well-being. Unregulated emotions affect not just you but your children in significant ways.

Adult children who grew up in an emotionally turbulent environment might struggle with their emotions, have difficulty forming healthy relationships, and be more prone to anxiety and depression. The patterns they learned in childhood can persist if not addressed.

The Impact of Culture and Family on Emotional Regulation

Culture is a powerful force shaping how we perceive and express emotions. In some cultures, it is customary to be reserved and avoid displaying negative emotions such as sadness or anger in public. On the other hand, in different cultures, emotional expressiveness is not just accepted; it is celebrated. Cultural expectations can make a huge difference in how children regulate their emotions. For example, some cultures value respect and obedience, which may lead children to suppress their emotions to avoid conflict. If your cultural background encourages emotional restraint, you must balance respect for tradition and promoting emotional expression within the family.

Cultural beliefs about emotions also play a crucial role in their regulation. In some cultures, emotions are perceived as dangerous and something to be controlled; others view them as a natural and healthy part of life. When you understand your cultural beliefs about emotions, you can help your child learn and thrive. Your family, especially you in your role as a parent, optimally affects your child's emotional regulation.

Imagine a child growing up in a culture where emotional expressiveness is highly valued. This child is likely to feel comfortable expressing both positive and negative emotions. On the other hand is a scenario where a child's emotions are not validated within the family, and they are often punished for expressing certain feelings. This child is more likely to suppress their emotions, which can lead to adverse outcomes such as anxiety, depression, and behavioral issues. In the same way, a child raised in a chaotic and stressful home environment and constantly exposed to stressful situations is likely to develop behavioral problems.

The ongoing stress can hinder their ability to learn how to manage their emotions effectively.

Different cultures have diverse ways of talking about emotions. Some cultures have a rich vocabulary for expressing them, while others might have a more limited range. This linguistic variation can affect how people understand and manage their emotions.

Cultural norms also influence how people cope with emotions. For instance, some cultures attribute emotions to external factors such as spirits or bad luck, while others view them as stemming from internal sources such as thoughts or beliefs. These perspectives can shape how you handle emotional regulation.

Cultural norms often dictate how you express your emotions in public. In some cultures, displaying negative emotions in public settings is considered impolite. These norms can influence how your child regulates their emotions in social situations.

Your parenting style can also contribute to your kids' emotional regulation or dysregulation. Parents who provide warmth and support create an environment where children are more likely to develop healthy emotional regulation skills. Children who feel loved and secure are better equipped to manage their emotions. On the other hand, adopting an authoritarian or punitive approach might inadvertently cause your children to fear your emotions. This fear can hinder the expression and management of emotions, leading to difficulties in emotional regulation.

The quality of your relationship with your child is another vital factor. If your children have close and secure bonds with you, they will likely develop better emotional regulation skills. By the same token, kids in insecure or ambivalent relationships can struggle with emotional regulation.

Trauma or abuse within the family can have a profound negative impact on emotional regulation. Children who experience trauma or abuse might associate their emotions with danger, affecting how they regulate their feelings, especially in stressful situations.

For example, if your culture considers it rude to display negative emotions in public, your child might learn to suppress their emotions outside the home. This suppression can make it difficult for them to express and manage their feelings effectively in social situations. Also, in a family with authoritarian parents, a child might fear expressing their emotions, leading to challenges in emotional regulation. If a child has experienced trauma or abuse, they might associate their emotions with danger. This association can hinder their ability to regulate their emotions during stressful circumstances.

Common Challenges to Emotional Regulation in Children

Some children are born with more intense temperaments. This means they might find it more challenging to regulate their emotions, especially when things get heated. Children with stronger temperaments can be more prone to tantrums, outbursts, and meltdowns. Additionally, they might find it difficult to calm down once they're upset. Temperament is a natural part of who your child is, and your role is to help them learn how to manage their emotions within the framework of their unique disposition.

Children with developmental delays might have difficulty regulating their emotions. This is because they might not possess the same cognitive or language skills as their peers, making it tough to express and understand their emotions effectively. Moreover, handling change and transitions might be especially challenging for them, often leading to emotional outbursts. In these situations, patience and tailored communication strategies can make a significant difference in helping your child cope.

Certain mental health disorders, such as anxiety and ADHD, can present additional challenges in emotional regulation. For instance, children with anxiety disorders often experience excessive worry and fear, leading to emotional outbursts. On the other hand, children with ADHD can struggle with impulse control and attention, which can also contribute to emotional difficulties. In such cases, early diagnosis and appropriate intervention are essential for your child's emotional well-being.

Physical factors like fatigue and hunger can also significantly affect your child's ability to regulate their emotions. When children are tired or hungry, they become more irritable and frustrated. This heightened emotional state can lead to outbursts or meltdowns.

Sensory Processing Disorder (SPD) struggles can affect the processing of sensory information effectively. This difficulty can make it especially hard for them to regulate their emotions. For example, a child with SPD might become overstimulated and have a meltdown in a crowded or noisy setting. Understanding and accommodating their sensory needs can significantly aid in emotional regulation.

Children with learning disabilities might face frustration and emotional outbursts, primarily when dealing with reading, writing, and math tasks. These challenges can lead to feelings of inadequacy and isolation, as they might perceive themselves as different from their peers. As a parent, providing extra support, encouragement, and tailored learning strategies can help alleviate some of these emotional struggles.

In addition, children with social-emotional problems might have difficulties interacting with others and managing their emotions in social situations. This can lead to feelings of isolation, rejection, and emotional turmoil. Additionally, these children could have trouble understanding and responding to others' emotions. Encouraging social interactions and teaching emotional awareness can be beneficial in such cases.

Emotional regulation challenges can significantly impact your child's life. Given these challenges, your understanding, support, and proactive engagement are invaluable. These challenges can manifest in various ways, affecting different aspects of their daily routine and interactions. Children aged 3-7 can struggle with managing their impulses without emotional regulation. They might act without thinking, resulting in behavioral problems and outbursts.

They can also find it challenging to adhere to rules and instructions. This difficulty can lead to frustration and emotional outbursts. Interacting positively with others, including peers and siblings, might also be a challenge, and the resulting conflict could result in social isolation and emotional problems.

Likewise, managing change and transitions can be particularly problematic for children in this age range. Being faced with new situations can lead to anxiety and emotional outbursts.

Something else to note is that some children are sensitive to sensory stimuli like noise, light, and other environmental factors. This sensitivity can make it challenging to regulate their emotions. Also, children who struggle with attention and concentration could find emotional regulation challenging. Their inability to recognize and respond to emotional cues can compound the issue.

The Basics of Dialectical Behavior Therapy (DBT) for Parents

Dialectical behavior therapy (DBT) is a type of psychotherapy Marsha Linehan developed in the 1980s to treat borderline personality disorder (BPD). It is a skills-based therapy that helps people learn how to regulate their emotions, tolerate distress, and improve their relationships. DBT teaches people skills in four key areas: mindfulness, distress tolerance, interpersonal effectiveness, and skills training.

Mindfulness is the ability to pay attention to the present moment without judgment. Better put, it's the ability to stay in the present situation and comprehend what is happening, including being aware of your thoughts, feelings, and sensations without getting caught up in them. Mindfulness can help you to regulate your emotions, cope with stress, and make better decisions.

Distress tolerance is the ability to cope with difficult emotions in a healthy way. This means finding ways to manage your emotions without resorting to destructive behaviors such as self-harm or substance abuse. Distress tolerance skills can help you stay calm in difficult situations and avoid making impulsive decisions.

Interpersonal effectiveness is the ability to communicate effectively and build healthy relationships. This means being able to clearly and assertively express needs and wants while also being respectful of the needs and wants of others. Interpersonal effectiveness skills can help you resolve conflicts, build trust, and meet your needs.

The last part of DBT is skills training, which is learning specific skills, such as problem-solving and emotion regulation, to manage BPD symptoms. This can involve learning how to identify your emotions, healthily express them, and cope with them if they're difficult. Skills training can help you manage your BPD symptoms and improve your quality of life.

As a parent, dialectical behavior therapy (DBT) can be pretty helpful in several ways. Learning the skills of DBT can help you regulate your emotions and cope with stress in a healthy way. You can also teach these skills to your children, helping them to regulate their emotions, tolerate distress, and improve their relationships. DBT principles can also help encourage positive interactions with your children, such as using mindfulness to stay present and aware of your emotions, using distress tolerance skills to cope with difficult emotions, and using interpersonal effectiveness skills to communicate effectively.

For example, if you are angry, you can use mindfulness skills to become more aware of the physical sensations of anger in your body and label your thoughts and feelings. You can then use distress tolerance skills to calm down, take deep breaths, or count to ten. Finally, you can use interpersonal effectiveness skills to clearly and calmly communicate your anger to your child.

If you're responding to your child's misbehavior, you can use mindfulness to stay present and aware of your emotions and distress tolerance skills to cope with your anger or frustration. Then, use interpersonal effectiveness skills to communicate clearly with your child in a calm manner about your expectations and the consequences of their misbehavior.

DBT for children, or DBT-C, is a special therapy is a special therapy designed for kids and teenagers who struggle with emotions. It is based on some pretty scientific ideas, but don't worry, it's all made kid-friendly. DBT-C is often done in a group with a trained therapist, which is useful because the kids can learn from each other and support each other. The group setting forms something like a team that's there to help your child grow emotionally. Sometimes, kids also have one-on-one sessions with a therapist to give them a chance to work on their specific challenges and get personalized help.

DBT-C can help with many things like ADHD, anxiety, mood issues, and even things like eating disorders or trauma. So, if your child is going through a tough time, DBT-C might be a great option.

DBT-C can be used alongside other therapies like family therapy or individual therapy. You might be thinking, "Is this really going to help my child?" Well, research has shown that DBT-C can be really effective. If your child often acts out, defies rules, or is just plain difficult, DBT-C can teach them better ways to handle their emotions and behavior. Kids with conduct disorder (CD) often have trouble often have trouble following rules and can be aggressive. DBT-C can help them find healthier ways to express themselves.

DBT-C can teach kids with ADHD how to better manage their impulses and emotions, and if your child struggles with anxiety or mood swings, DBT-C can help handle these big feelings. For kids dealing with food and body image issues, or if your child has been through a tough or scary experience, DBT-C can help them process those feelings and move forward.

The Science of Emotions: A Parent's Guide

The science of emotions is a fast-growing discipline with fresh insights into how children's emotions grow. As a parent, understanding your children's emotions can help you secure their emotional well-being.

One of the key findings of the science of emotions is that emotions are not simply internal states. Our conduct, body language, and facial expressions can communicate them. This implies that our emotions might strongly impact our relationships with others.

Another important finding of the science of emotions is that emotions are not always negative. We all know that emotions such as joy and love can be positive and adaptive. The flip side is that even negative emotions such as sadness and anger can serve a purpose. For example, sadness can help us to grieve a loss, while anger can motivate us to act against injustice.

Emotions are essential for children's healthy development. They help your children understand the world around them, communicate with others, and regulate their behavior. You might be unable to figure out what is in your kid's mind if they do not occasionally display their emotions. You can help your children to develop healthy emotional intelligence by talking to them about their emotions. Name and label your child's emotions and discuss the situations that trigger them.

You should also learn to validate their feelings. Let your child know it's okay to feel negative emotions. Help them cope with difficult emotions and teach them healthy ways to manage them. One easy way to do this is by modeling healthy emotional expression. Children learn by watching adults, and you can set a good example of how to express your emotions healthily. You can also ensure they have a supportive environment for emotional development: Your children need to feel safe and loved to thrive emotionally.

You play a big role in helping your children develop healthy emotional intelligence. One of the most important things parents can do is help their children develop emotional self-awareness. This means helping them to identify, label, and understand their emotions. You can do this by talking to your children about their feelings, reading books about emotions, and playing games that involve expressing emotions (Margot 2016). Once children are aware of their emotions, they can develop emotional regulation skills. This means learning how to manage their emotions, and you can make this easier by teaching them relaxation techniques, problem-solving strategies, and coping mechanisms.

Building Emotional Awareness: Mindfulness Techniques

You are emotionally aware when you can identify and understand your emotions and those of others. That might seem pretty straightforward — it's easy to differentiate anger from pain, right? — but emotional awareness goes beyond recognizing primary emotions. It's about thoroughly understanding even the subtle differences between similar feelings like annoyance and frustration or caring and understanding.

To get better at this, you can use helpful mindfulness techniques to help you build emotional awareness by increasing attention to bodily sensations. Mindfulness involves noticing the physical sensations associated with different emotions such as tightness in the chest or a racing heart. This tactic can help you identify emotions more quickly and accurately.

When practicing mindfulness, you also learn to reduce your emotional reactivity. Mindfulness teaches you to observe emotions without getting caught up in them. This can help you to avoid impulsive reactions and make more thoughtful choices. Paying attention to your emotions also helps you gain a greater understanding of emotional triggers, something that can be used to develop coping mechanisms and avoid emotional overload. Mindfulness also involves being kind and accepting of yourself even when feeling difficult emotions: You're only human.

Don't chicken out yet! Mindfulness techniques can be practiced in any place at any time, individually or in a group setting. With regular practice, mindfulness can help you become a pro at emotional awareness, which can be beneficial for you and your kids.

Take mindful breathing, for example. This technique involves paying attention to the breath entering and exiting the body. When you do this, you calm your mind and focus attention on the present moment. This particular skill works well for me.

What if I told you there is such a thing as mindful walking, where you can develop your emotional awareness and get some exercise while you're at it. Impressive, right? Mindful walking also increases awareness of the body and the surrounding environment. You get to better appreciate the beauty of nature while calmly examining the emotions you feel at that moment. There is also mindful journaling, writing about thoughts, feelings, and experiences non-judgmentally. This can also help you keep track of your emotional progression.

See? It's not that hard. Mindfulness is quite beneficial, and you can reap its amazing benefits once you put your mind to it.

Identifying Triggers and Emotional Responses

One thing I really enjoy watching is "Card Cascade." Rows of cards standing upright are arranged together, one next to the other, perfectly balanced. It usually takes a push to knock out the first card, which knocks out the next, the next, and the next until the whole arrangement crumbles. It's quite satisfying to watch, and it reminds me in a way of how a little emotional trigger can lead to cascades of emotional response. For example, if you try to get your child to bed after a long day but she wants to watch more TV, you can become very angry, and other emotions, such as frustration, sadness, or anxiety, can spill out. Your spiraling emotions, in turn, trigger your child, who begins to cry, which gets you even angrier, and then the cycle continues.

One key thing that can take your parenting from zero to ten is being emotionally intelligent, and you can do that by identifying triggers and emotional responses. Trauma can leave us hypersensitive to certain situations or circumstances and trigger emotional reactions that make it seem like you are overreacting. These triggers can be internal, such as thoughts or memories; or external, such as people, places, or objects. Once you know your triggers, you can develop strategies for mastering them.

So, how do you identify your triggers? Start by paying more attention to situations, words, or actions that set you off. What are the things that get you very angry, sad, anxious, or scared? Once you identify those triggers, find out exactly how they make you feel, and that is emotional awareness. You can also think about the thoughts that go through your mind when you're triggered. How did you respond to the situation?

You might not have control of your triggers, but you can determine your emotional response, which is key. How you respond emotionally to your child's behavior can greatly impact your parenting relationship and your child's emotional development. Rather than responding impulsively, you can train yourself to respond emotionally in the best way possible. It's also important to learn to detach the situation from the person: For example, your child is not "stupid" just because they made a stupid decision.

Walk away from the situation. If you can, take a few minutes to cool down before you respond. You can also practice communication and talk to your child about how you feel; this can help them understand why you are reacting the way you are and learn how to behave in a less triggering way.

Embracing Emotions: Validation and Acceptance

We all want to raise children who are emotionally healthy and well-adjusted, and one way to do that is to teach them to embrace their emotions. This means validating and accepting their feelings, even when it's difficult. Validation means acknowledging and accepting. When teaching your kids to embrace their emotions, tell them their feelings are real and that they are okay to feel that way. Let your child know that it's okay to be sad or upset, even angry. When you validate your children's emotions, you tell them that you care about them and understand how they feel.

Validation is necessary because it helps children feel safe and supported. They are less likely to feel overwhelmed or alone when they know their feelings are accepted. Also, validation helps children learn how to manage their emotions. If they know their feelings are okay, they are more likely to talk about them and find better ways to handle them.

There are many ways to validate your child's emotions. You can acknowledge their feelings by saying, "I see that you're angry." You should focus on using non-judgmental language and avoid saying things like, "You shouldn't feel that way." Empathize with them, letting them know you understand how they feel. You can even give them examples of situations that made you feel the way they currently do. You don't have to be quick to try and fix their feelings; just let them know you are there for them.

That is where acceptance comes in. Acceptance means not trying to change or make them feel bad for feeling the way they do. When you accept your children's emotions, you're showing them that you love and respect them, even when they are imperfect. Even as adults, we appreciate being accepted by our spouse or loved ones even when we do not act very okay with our feelings.

To make accepting your kid's emotions easier, remember that emotions are temporary. Your son or daughter will not always be sad or overly excited. You should also avoid taking your child's emotions personally. I learned this a long time ago, and it really helped me. Their feelings do not reflect upon you or your parenting, and their emotional responses have more to do with who *they* are than who *you* are. Give them space to feel their emotions; don't try to force them to bottle up or provide a quick fix. Instead, teach them to ride the waves of their emotions responsibly. Rather than bottling things up, help them find healthy ways to express their emotions including talking, writing, or exercising.

Practical Worksheet: My Emotional Journal

Date: _____ Time: _____

Emotion Check-In

Today, I felt:

(Describe your emotions. Were you happy, sad, excited, angry, anxious, or something else? Be specific.)

Emotion	Description

Why I felt this way:

(What happened or what was the trigger for these emotions? Try to identify the specific event or thought.)

Emotion	Trigger or Event

How intense were my emotions?

(On a scale from 1 to 10, with 1 being very mild and 10 being extremely intense, rate the intensity of each emotion.)

Emotion	Intensity (1-10)

How did I react to my emotions?

(Describe how you responded to your feelings. Did you talk to someone, keep it to yourself, or take any specific actions?)

- Talked to a friend or family member.
- Wrote about it in my journal.
- Did a creative activity (e.g., drawing, painting).
- Practiced deep breathing.
- Listened to music.
- Engaged in physical activity (e.g., exercise, dance).

What did I learn from this emotional experience?

(Reflect on what you learned about yourself or your emotions from today's experiences.)

Emotion	Lesson Learned

What can I do to manage or cope with these emotions in the future?

(Think about strategies or activities that might help you deal with similar feelings if they arise.)

- Practice meditation.
- Create a gratitude list.
- Reach out to a counselor or therapist.
- Try a new relaxation technique.
- Talk to a trusted adult or friend.

Takeaway One

- Unregulated emotions can significantly impact children's development and well-being.
- You can help your children learn to regulate their emotions by modeling healthy emotional regulation, teaching them about emotions, and helping them develop coping mechanisms for dealing with difficult emotions.
- Dialectical behavior therapy (DBT) is a type of psychotherapy that can help people learn how to regulate their emotions, tolerate distress, and improve their relationships.
- DBT can be used in parenting in a few ways. The four keys of DBT are mindfulness, distress tolerance, interpersonal effectiveness, and skills training.
- Emotional triggers are the events, people, or situations that cause us to feel strong emotions such as anger, sadness, or anxiety.

- How you respond emotionally to your triggers can greatly impact your mental and physical health and relationships.
- It is important to validate and accept your children's emotions. This means letting them know that their feelings are real and that they are okay to feel that way.

CHAPTER TWO

Mastering Anger Management

"The Golden Rule of Parenting is do unto your children as you wish your parents had done unto you!"

— **Louise Hart**

"Better a patient person than a warrior, one with self-control than one who takes a city."

— **Proverbs 16:32 (NKJV)**

Tererai Trent grew up in a small village in Zimbabwe; she faced a difficult upbringing due to her father's harsh and unpredictable temper. His anger made her feel unsafe and caused her to retreat to her room in fear. This experience led to a deep sense of insecurity and self-doubt and made her feel inadequate and unworthy. As a result, Tererai struggled with a constant feeling of not being good enough.

A study conducted by researchers at the University of California, Los Angeles, followed a group of children from birth to age 18. The researchers found that children exposed to high levels of parental anger were more likely to develop anxiety and depression symptoms at age 18, even after controlling for other factors such as the child's temperament and family income (Davies *et al.* 2007).

The study also found that these kids were more likely to have relationship problems and difficulty regulating their emotions. For example, they were more likely to have difficulty making friends, get into fights, and have difficulty controlling their anger.

A similar study found that children exposed to parental anger were more likely to engage in aggressive behavior at school such as fighting and bullying. These kids were also more likely to have problems in school and difficulty forming healthy relationships. They were more likely to have low academic achievement, to get into trouble with the law, and to have difficulty maintaining friendships (Shaw *et al.* 2004).

Understanding the Physiology of Anger

Like all emotions, anger is not just a mental experience; it also affects our bodies. To understand anger's physiology, we have to start with the brain. In the brain, there are two almond-shaped structures called the amygdala. These regions are the emotional hubs responsible for detecting threats. When the amygdala senses a threat, it sets off an alarm, prompting us to take action to protect ourselves. What is intriguing and sometimes disturbing is that the amygdala operates swiftly, often faster than the cortex, the part of our brain responsible for rational thinking and judgment. In simple terms, our brains are wired to react before we can fully think through the consequences of our actions.

This is not an excuse for unruly behavior but rather proof that managing anger is a necessary parenting skill. We are not born knowing how to do this, so you must practice it.

As things get heated, your muscles tense up, and the brain releases neurotransmitters known as catecholamine, giving you a rush of energy that lasts several minutes. This surge of energy makes you want to act quickly and, most likely, irrationally. Simultaneously, your heart beats faster, your blood pressure rises, and your breathing becomes faster. Your face might even flush as increased blood flow rushes to your limbs and extremities in preparation for physical action. Your attention becomes laser-focused on the source of your anger, making it nearly impossible to concentrate on anything else. At this point, your body is primed for a fight.

However, it is important to note that our brain has a counterbalance to anger, the prefrontal cortex. While the amygdala handles emotions, the prefrontal cortex is responsible for judgment and can "switch off" your emotional response. Managing anger effectively means finding ways to help your prefrontal cortex gain control over your amygdala, allowing you to decide how you react to anger. Techniques like relaxation can reduce arousal and decrease amygdala activity, while cognitive control methods help you use judgment to override emotional reactions.

If anger has a physiological preparation phase, when our bodies gear up for a fight, it also has a wind-down phase. When the target of our anger is no longer a threat, our bodies gradually return to a resting state. However, this relaxation process is somewhat tough because the adrenaline-induced arousal triggered by anger can last for hours or even days. It lowers our anger threshold, making it easier to become angry over minor irritations that would typically not bother us. During this slow cooldown period, our ability to remember details of the angry outburst might also be impaired. Arousal is essential for effective memory, but excessive arousal, such as what we experience when we're angry, can hinder the formation of new memories and decrease concentration. This is why we often struggle to recall specifics from heated arguments.

Now, let's talk about anger in the context of your child. Children, like adults, undergo physiological changes when they experience anger. Their bodies might exhibit signs such as increased energy, raised blood pressure, hormonal spikes (adrenaline and noradrenaline), higher body temperature, muscle tension, and various outward expressions like raised voices, clenched fists, frowning, a clenched jaw, trembling, rapid heartbeats, sweating, and pacing.

While anger is a normal part of growing up, chronic or uncontrolled anger in children can lead to emotional and physical health issues. Help your child learn how to manage anger constructively to avoid future complications. Teaching your child to understand and regulate their physiological responses to anger is essential for their overall well-being.

When we experience anger, our bodies undergo various biological and physiological changes. These changes are part of the body's stress response and can include:

Increased Blood Pressure: Anger often goes hand in hand with a spike in blood pressure. This elevation in blood pressure directly results from your body's response to the perceived threat. While this heightened state is useful in emergencies, prolonged or frequent anger episodes can place added strain on your cardiovascular system. Over time, this strain may contribute to serious health issues, including heart disease and stroke.

Release of Hormones: The hormonal response to anger is profound. Hormones like adrenaline and noradrenaline surge into your bloodstream. These chemicals are like emotional amplifiers, intensifying your emotional state and making you feel more alert and ready for action. They prepare your body to confront a threat, whether real or perceived.

Increased Body Temperature: Anger can cause your body temperature to rise. This temperature rise results from the heightened physiological response to the emotion. It reflects the increased metabolic activity when your body prepares for a fight-or-flight response. This elevated temperature is one of the many ways your body reacts to anger.

Increased Muscle Tension: Increased muscle tension is another common physical manifestation of anger. Your muscles tighten and contract as a part of your body's preparation for action. This can manifest as clenched fists, a clenched jaw, or even trembling in more severe cases. This is your body's way of gearing up for potential physical confrontation.

Physical Symptoms: The physiological changes associated with anger can manifest in visible physical symptoms. These outward signs can include raised voices, frowns, rapid heartbeats, excessive sweating, pacing, and more. They are visible indicators of your emotional state and can impact how others perceive and respond to your anger.

Depression: Uncontrolled anger can increase the risk of developing depression, characterized by persistent sadness, hopelessness, and a loss of interest in activities you once enjoyed.

Anxiety: Chronic anger can exacerbate anxiety disorders, increasing worry, restlessness, and heightening stress levels.

Insomnia: Anger-related stress can disrupt your sleep patterns, resulting in insomnia and its associated health problems. Adequate sleep is essential for overall health, so addressing anger-related sleep disturbances is vital.

Gastric Ulcers: The physical and emotional strain of anger can contribute to the development of gastrointestinal problems such as gastric ulcers. These conditions can cause discomfort and impact your digestive health.

Bowel Disease: Prolonged stress resulting from unresolved anger might be linked to developing or exacerbating bowel diseases.

Diabetes: The relationship between chronic anger, stress, and diabetes is complex. However, evidence suggests that ongoing anger and stress contribute to the risk of developing diabetes. It underscores the importance of addressing anger for overall health.

The Psychology of Anger

Anger is not an emotion in isolation; it is closely linked to pain. Whenever we feel anger, it is almost always preceded by some form of pain. This pain can take various forms such as feeling rejected, threatened, or experiencing a loss. The type of pain does not matter; what matters is that it is unpleasant.

However, pain alone is not enough to trigger anger. Anger surfaces when pain combines with certain thoughts or interpretations. These thoughts can be personal assumptions, evaluations, or perceptions that lead us to believe someone is intentionally trying to hurt us. Anger is a social emotion — there is always a target our anger is directed toward, even if that target happens to be ourselves. The fusion of pain and anger-triggering thoughts motivate you to take action, confront perceived threats, and protect yourself by reacting to the source of your pain.

Interestingly, anger can also act as a substitute emotion. People sometimes intentionally make themselves angry as a way to avoid feeling pain. This transformation from pain to anger can occur consciously or unconsciously. Why do we do this? Because, for many, anger feels more manageable and less vulnerable than pain.

When we are in pain, our natural inclination is to focus on that pain. But when we become angry, our attention shifts from self-focus to other-focus. We start thinking about how to retaliate against those we perceive are causing us pain. In this way, anger acts as a smokescreen, shielding us from the reality of feeling frightened or vulnerable.

Moreover, anger offers several benefits, including distraction and a sense of righteousness, power, and moral superiority that pain does not provide. When we are angry, we believe we have a just cause. We begin to think, "The people who hurt me are wrong; they should be punished." It is rare for someone to become angry with someone they do not believe has significantly harmed them in some way.

The assessment of whether someone's anger is problematic often hinges on whether others agree that their anger and the actions driven by that anger are justified. Angry people usually fervently believe that their anger is entirely justified. However, the perspectives of others can significantly impact the consequences faced by the person expressing the anger.

Justified or not, anger can lead to real-life consequences. An angry person might feel that their aggressive actions are warranted, but legal consequences can follow if judges or peers do not see it that way. You can even lose your job if your boss deems anger toward a customer unjustified, and relationships can become strained if your spouse disagrees with the anger's justification.

Whether or not our anger is justified, it carries a seductive sense of righteousness, temporarily boosting our self-esteem. It feels better to be angry than to acknowledge the painful feelings associated with vulnerability.

Furthermore, anger allows us to convert feelings of vulnerability and helplessness into feelings of control and power. Some people unconsciously develop a habit of turning almost all of their vulnerable feelings into anger to avoid addressing them directly.

To truly grasp anger's dynamics, we must consider its stages. This can help us manage it effectively and recognize when to intervene before anger escalates beyond control.

1. **Getting Triggered:** This initial stage marks the starting point. Anger always has a trigger, which can be either external or internal. External triggers can include events or situations in our environment, such as someone cutting you off in traffic or receiving a curt reply from a colleague. On the other hand, internal triggers originate from our thoughts and emotions. For example, you can become angry when you interpret someone's actions as disrespectful or threatening.

2. **Buildup of Anger:** After the initial trigger, our minds construct a narrative that justifies our anger. This internal story often

intensifies our anger, making it more difficult to release. You replay the triggering event in your mind; at this point, your anger builds like a pressure cooker. You still have some capacity to reassess the situation during this stage. It is an opportunity to question the validity of your anger and whether it aligns with the facts surrounding the situation.

3. **Preparing for Action:** Your body prepares for action as anger escalates. This is where the fight-or-flight response kicks in. Muscles become tense, pupils dilate to absorb more information, nostrils flare to allow more air, breathing quickens to oxygenate our bodies, and heart rate increases to provide more energy. In this stage, you become physiologically primed for action. Rational thinking becomes increasingly challenging as our body's survival instincts take over.

4. **Feeling the Impulse to Act:** The buildup of anger generates a powerful impulse to act, often aggressively. This impulse is intended to release the pent-up energy within us like a pressure valve that's ready to burst. The urge to express our anger becomes almost irresistible.

5. **Acting on the Anger:** This stage is where anger reaches its peak and we take action. Unfortunately, rational thinking is often elusive at this point. We can begin to act hostile and aggressive as we act on our anger. At this stage, we might say or do things we later regret.

6. **Relief:** There is a moment of temporary relief after acting on our anger as if a pressure valve has been opened, and the intense emotions are temporarily unburdened. This relief can be

deceptive, as it can lead us to believe that expressing anger is the solution. However, this relief is short-lived, and the underlying issues that triggered the anger often remain unresolved.

7. **Recovery:** After the anger outburst, you cool down. This stage involves a return to a more rational and composed state. However, you experience complex emotions during this phase such as guilt, shame, regret, or depression. You reflect on your behavior during the anger episode, which might feel like a force temporarily possessed you.

8. **Repair:** You reflect and learn in this final stage. This is when you assess your behavior and its impact on others. If your anger harms relationships or situations, you might feel compelled to apologize and make amends.

The Angry Parent Trap: Common Triggers

Case Study

Sarah and Tom sat at the kitchen table, the stacks of bills and unopened mail before them reminding them of their financial situation. It's not like they're poor, but things haven't been this bad in a long while. And every little expense pushes them further into debt.

Their children's laughter drifted in from the living room. It's a sound that usually warmed their heart, but tonight, it just reminded them of the crushing weight of responsibility.

They were still reflecting on this when they heard a loud crash, followed by a louder cry of pain from their youngest son. They rushed into the living room to find Lily standing over her brother, a guilty expression on her face. Sarah's beloved ceramic vase was in pieces beside him.

"What happened?" Sarah demanded, her voice sharp with anger as she scooped Nathan up.

Tom, on the other hand, on seeing how much his son was bleeding, kept thinking about how much an emergency room visit would cost. He banged his fists on the wall in frustration.

"I-I didn't mean to." Lily stuttered, tears rolling down her cheeks. "It was an accident."

"Let's bandage his wounds," Sarah said to Tom. She saw the fear in her children's eyes and knew that their outbursts only made things worse.

It is a no-brainer that many parents struggle with anger. Anger is a normal human emotion, but it can be especially difficult to manage when you are a parent. Your children constantly push your buttons, test your limits, and make you crazy. It is very easy to lose your temper now and then. The good news is that there are things you can do to manage your anger and avoid getting caught in the angry parent trap. One good way to begin is by identifying your triggers. These are the things that get you angry and worked up.

One common anger trigger is stress. It's quite easy to become overwhelmed, making it difficult to control your emotions. Stress puts you on edge, making you like a hot pot of coffee ready to boil over at any moment. This can lead to anger outbursts, even if you would not normally react this way. Another trigger closely related to that is feeling tired or sleep-deprived. When you're not well-rested, you get grumpy and edgy, making it easy to lose your temper. This is because lack of sleep can impair your judgment and make it more difficult to regulate your emotions.

Feelings of frustration and hopelessness can also put you at risk of anger outbursts. Feeling like you cannot control a situation can be frustrating and easily degenerate into anger. This is especially common when dealing with children, as they can be unpredictable and difficult to manage. Criticism is also another common trigger. No one likes to be criticized or judged, and this can be especially true for parents. When you feel like you are being criticized, it can trigger your anger and make it difficult to stay calm. The same goes for when you are hurt or rejected. This is especially common when your child does something that hurts you, such as saying something mean or disobeying you.

If you find yourself getting angry easily, it is important to identify your triggers so that you can start to manage them. Once you know what triggers your anger, you can start to develop strategies for coping in a healthy way.

DBT Skills for Anger: Distress Tolerance

As parents, we all experience moments of anger and frustration. Dealing with our anger can be as hard as helping our children manage theirs. This is where distress tolerance skills come into play, and they can be invaluable for us parents, too. Distress tolerance skills are designed to help people cope with difficult emotions in a healthy manner. They can help manage anger, anxiety, sadness, and other difficult emotions.

Let's start with self-soothing techniques. When you feel overwhelmed or stressed, find ways to calm yourself down. Just like kids have comfort items, adults have ways to self-soothe, too. You should also learn to weigh the pros and cons of your actions. In the heat of the moment, you can make impulsive decisions driven by your emotions. Make a quick mental note of your decision's potential advantages and disadvantages. This simple exercise can help you see the bigger picture and make more balanced choices.

Sometimes, you cannot control a situation, and trying to do so only adds to your frustration. In these situations, you need to practice radical acceptance. Radical acceptance means acknowledging that some things are beyond your control. It is a way of saying, "It is what it is." Letting go of the need to control everything can ease your stress and reduce emotional turmoil.

When you find yourself overwhelmed, consider temporary distractions. Shift your focus to something unrelated to the source of your distress. It could be a call to a friend, watching a TV show, reading a book, spending time with pets, or any activity that redirects your mind. Distraction provides a mental breathing space.

Sometimes, our emotions become so overwhelming that it is challenging to regain control. Think of it as your emotional "system" overheating and freezing up. To get back on track, consider TIPP skills. TIPP stands for Temperature, Intense Exercise, Paced Breathing, and Paired Muscle Relaxation. These skills work swiftly to calm the emotional storm. They are easy to practice anywhere and do not have any side effects like medication does.

Temperature:

Sudden exposure to cold water can send shock waves to your system, helping you snap out of your intense emotional state. Splash cold water on your face, take a cold shower, or hold ice cubes in your hands.

Intense Exercise:

Physical activity, especially intense exercise, can positively change your body chemistry. Think of it as channeling your energy and frustration and maintaining a nice shape.

Paced Breathing:

Breathing exercises give you a sense of control. Breathe slowly through your nose for two counts, hold for three counts, and exhale slowly through your mouth for five counts. This helps lower your blood pressure and promotes relaxation.

Paired Muscle Relaxation (PMR):

As you breathe in and out, tense and then relax pairs of muscles while breathing in and out. It relaxes your body and calms your mind, strengthening the mind-body connection.

Cognitive Restructuring for Parental Anger

Another useful skill is cognitive behavioral therapy (CBT), which helps you identify and challenge negative thoughts about yourself, others, and even the world. When you get angry, you tend to think negatively about your children, yourself, or the situation. These thoughts can make you feel angry, frustrated, and resentful. Cognitive restructuring can help you identify and replace negative thoughts with brighter, helpful ones: out with the old and in with the new.

For example, you might think, "My child is so lazy. They never do anything I ask them to do." That might be true, but maintaining that line of thought can lead to feelings of anger and frustration. However, if you were to challenge this thought and replace it with "My child is very helpful. They just need more time to get started," it could make you less angry and prevent unwanted emotional responses.

If you struggle with anger, cognitive restructuring can be very helpful as it can help you identify and challenge your negative thoughts about yourself and your children. CBT can also help you learn to think more rationally and realistically and develop helpful coping mechanisms for dealing with anger.

So, how exactly does CBT work? As we discussed earlier, you need to identify the negative thoughts and what is sponsoring them. Once you have done that, pay attention to your body language and physical sensations. When you are angry, you might notice that your body tenses, your heart rate increases, and your breathing becomes shallow. These physical sensations can be a clue that you are just about to have a barrage of negative thoughts or already have them.

You should also pay attention to your thoughts. When you're angry, try to pay attention to the thoughts going through your mind. What are you telling yourself about yourself, your child, or the situation? Ask yourself, "What am I telling myself that makes me angry?" This can help you identify the negative thoughts causing your anger.

Once you do that, challenge the negative thought, ask yourself questions about the thought, and look for evidence to support or refute it. For example, if you think, "My child is so lazy," you could ask yourself, "What evidence do I have for this? Have they ever done anything helpful?" You could also ask yourself, "What are other possible explanations for why my child is not doing what I ask them to do?"

Once you have challenged the negative thought, you can replace it with a more helpful thought. This new thought should be accurate and realistic. For example, if you think, "My child is so lazy," you could replace that thought with, "My child is still learning to follow instructions. They need more time and patience."

The final step is to practice the new thought. This means thinking about it regularly and using it to challenge your negative thoughts when they arise. The more you practice the new thought, the more likely you are to believe it, and the less likely you are to feel angry.

Communication Strategies to Prevent Explosions

When you put food in a pressure cooker, steam builds inside. If the pressure gets too high, the cooker will explode. Anger is like the steam in the pressure cooker. When we experience something that makes us angry, the anger builds inside of us. It can eventually explode if we do not find a healthy way to express our anger. An explosion can be destructive. It can hurt people and damage property. Anger can also be destructive. It can damage relationships, ruin careers, and even lead to violence.

So, how can you prevent an explosion? The same way we prevent a pressure cooker from exploding. You need to find a way to release the steam, and you can start by being assertive. Assertiveness is communicating and expressing your needs and opinions clearly and directly without being aggressive or passive. When you're assertive, you can stand up for yourself without being aggressive or disrespectful.

Active listening can also be helpful, meaning paying attention to what the other person is saying verbally and nonverbally. It also means understanding their point of view and trying to see things from their perspective. When you listen actively, you are more likely to be able to constructively resolve conflict. Use "I" statements. "I" statements communicate your feelings and needs without blaming or attacking the other person, in this case, your kids. To use "I" statements, start by saying "I" and then describe your feelings and the specific behavior that bothers you. For example, you could say, "I feel angry when you do not put your dishes away."

How about taking a break? If you're feeling angry, it's important to take a break before you say or do anything you might regret. Take some time to cool down and calm yourself down before you continue the conversation. If you say or do something you regret, apologizing is important. A sincere apology can help repair the relationship, prevent anger from escalating, and can be helpful to your kids' mental health.

Also, be aware of your triggers. We've discussed that already, but it is extremely important and worth another mention. What typically makes you angry? Once you know your triggers, you can avoid them or develop coping mechanisms for dealing with them.

Take care of yourself. You can better manage your anger when you're well-rested, healthy, and happy. Make sure to get enough sleep, eat healthy foods, and exercise regularly. Stress can be a major trigger for anger, so finding healthy ways to manage stress is important. This can include exercise, relaxation techniques, or spending time outside. Holding on to anger and resentment can harm your mental and physical health. Learn to forgive yourself and your kids for mistakes.

Teaching Your Child Healthy Anger Management

You need time to process your feelings after becoming upset. Even after the issue has been resolved or you have received an apology, you might still be upset, and that is all right. Learning how to manage emotions, especially strong ones like rage, can be pretty hard for kids, especially younger ones. Children can better respond to the emotions and surroundings around them if they learn to understand their feelings and develop emotional regulation skills.

For kids, anger is a tough emotion. They could feel the want to damage objects or say hurtful things. However, with the right tools and techniques, even young children can be taught to see anger differently and maintain or regain control over how they feel. As a parent, teaching your children healthy anger management skills will do you and them a lot of good, both in the heat of the moment and in the long run.

Talk to your child about anger. Explain that anger is a normal emotion but that it is important to express it in a healthy way. Talk about what anger feels like and how it can be expressed positively. Help your child identify their triggers: This works just about the same way as it does for you. What are the things that typically make your child angry? Once you know your child's triggers, you can help them avoid them or develop coping mechanisms for dealing with them.

You can also teach your child relaxation techniques, which can help calm them down when they are angry. You can teach them deep breathing, counting to ten, or taking a break from the situation.

The best way to teach your kids how to manage their anger is to model healthy anger management. As we've mentioned, children learn by watching adults. If you want your child to learn healthy anger management skills, model these skills for them. Try to stay calm and healthily express your anger when you are angry.

You can also set limits and expectations. Let your child know what behavior is acceptable and what is not. Be clear about the consequences of aggressive or destructive behavior. Help your child develop problem-solving skills. Teach your child how to deal calmly and assertively with difficult situations. Let your child know that it's okay to feel angry, but that they need to express it in a way that does not hurt themselves or others.

When they do well enough, give them a thumbs up. Praise them well when they use the techniques you have taught them. This will help them to learn that these skills are important and worth using.

Guided Visualization for Anger Release

Anger management and pain management have many similarities. They are both strong, prolonged feelings that you can find yourself obsessing about.

If you keep ruminating, reconsidering, reliving, or rehashing an occurrence that made you angry long after it happened, you will simplify the emotion. At first, you might just be irritated, but the more you think and talk about it, the angrier you become. You cannot let go of your thoughts or your feelings — you're trapped!

So, how can you get out of this rut? Try using guided visualization to direct your focus to something more pleasant. Guided visualization is a powerful tool for anger release. However, it's not a magic bullet. It takes time and practice to learn how to use it effectively. Here is how to get started in six easy steps:

1. Find a quiet place where you and your child will not be disturbed. Sit or lie down in a comfortable position. Close your eyes and take a few deep breaths.

2. Visualize a calming environment, such as a beach, a forest, or a meadow. Pay attention to the sights, sounds, and smells of this place.

3. As you visualize this calming environment, allow yourself and your child to relax and let go of any tension in your bodies.

4. If you or your child start to feel angry, remind yourself and your child that you are safe and in control. Visualize the anger leaving your body and being replaced by peace and calm.

5. Continue visualizing for as long as you like. When you're ready, open your eyes and take a few deep breaths.

6. You can also create a guided visualization. Start by thinking about a calming environment that you and your child enjoy. Then, add specific details, such as this place's sights, sounds, and smells.

Practical Worksheet: My Anger Control Plan

Anger is a natural and powerful emotion. Various situations and circumstances can trigger it, and as parents, there are moments when anger feels overwhelming. This practical worksheet is designed to help you create your personalized Anger Control Plan, a set of strategies and techniques you can use to manage your anger constructively. Let's get started.

1. Take a moment to reflect on the last few times you felt angry. What were the situations or events that triggered your anger?

2. List the physical signs you experience when you're angry. These could include things like increased heart rate, clenched fists, or shallow breathing.

    1. _____

    2. _____

    3. _____

    4. _____

    5. _____

    6. _____

3. Describe the emotions that accompany your anger. Are they frustrated, irritated, or something else?

_____

_____

_____

_____

_____

4. Identify the common situations or events that trigger your anger. Things like stress, lack of sleep, certain people, or specific circumstances.

    1. _____

2. _____

3. _____

4. _____

5. _____

6. _____

5. What early warning signs tell you when you start feeling angry? These can be subtle cues that signal the need for anger management.

_____
_____
_____
_____
_____
_____

6. Do you notice any patterns in your anger triggers? Are there specific times of the day or recurring situations when anger tends to arise?

7. Write down a simple breathing exercise you can use to calm yourself when anger arises. For example, "Take five slow, deep breaths: inhaling for a count of four, holding for a count of four, and exhaling for a count of six."

1. _____

2. _____

3. _____

4. _____

5. _____

6. _____

8. Create a list of positive affirmations or statements you can repeat to yourself when angry. For instance, "I can handle this situation calmly" or "I choose to respond, not react."

1. _____

2. _____

3. _____

4. _____

5. _____

6. _____

9. List healthy ways to release built-up anger. These can include physical activities like jogging, journaling, or talking to a trusted friend or family member.

_____

_____

_____

_____

10. Commit to regularly practicing your anger control strategies even when you're not angry. This helps you become more proficient in using them when needed.

Takeaway Two

- Distress tolerance is the ability to cope with difficult emotions healthily.

- Cognitive restructuring is a therapy that helps you change how you think about things. This can be helpful for anger management as it can help you to challenge negative thoughts and beliefs that contribute to anger.

- For example, if you think, "My child is always misbehaving," you could challenge this thought by saying, "My child is misbehaving sometimes, but they are also a good kid."

- It is important to teach your child healthy anger management skills from a young age. Talk to them about anger.

- Explain what anger is and how it feels. Help your child identify their triggers. Teach your child relaxation techniques such as deep breathing or counting to ten. Model healthy anger management skills. Be patient and understanding.

PART TWO
Parenting with DBT and Coping Skills

The first time I heard about DBT, I thought it was just another DIY quick fix. However, I took it upon myself to study and go through research and publications just to have a rounded perspective.

Parenting can be a challenging and stressful experience, and DBT skills can help you cope with the demands of parenthood. DBT stands for dialectical behavior therapy. It's a type of therapy that teaches skills for managing emotions, regulating behavior, and tolerating distress. DBT is effective for many mental health conditions, including borderline personality disorder, bipolar disorder, and eating disorders.

When you learn and practice DBT skills, you can develop greater emotional resilience, effective communication techniques, and a deeper understanding of your children's needs and behaviors. DBT-C, a specific form of DBT, instructs extensively on validating and creating a change-ready environment for your children. It also prepares you to become a coach for your child while teaching effective coping and problem-solving skills. Dialectical behavior therapy provides specific interventions to decrease vulnerabilities in the core senses of self-love, safety, and belonging.

This part will explore all you need to know about parenting with DBT with a focus on fostering a calm parenting style, age-appropriate mindfulness, coping techniques, and how to nurture a more open connection with your child.

I wrote this just for you; may it bless you as much as I hope it will.

CHAPTER THREE
Anxiety Coping Skills for Parents

"Worrying is like sitting in a rocking chair. It gives you something to do but doesn't get you anywhere."

— Erma Bombeck

"God is our refuge and strength, A very present help in trouble."

— Psalms 46:1 (NKJV)

Case Study

Mark wakes before the sun every morning. And every morning, he lays in bed for hours, worrying about a lot of things. Bills, work, his child's health, not being the kind of dad his child deserves, and feelings of impending doom.

And every morning that he drags himself out of the bed and into the kitchen, he worries about facing another day.

This morning is no different. His heart rate quickened with every passing moment, but as usual, he kept a brave façade for the sake of his family.

"Good morning, Dad," his daughter Emily said as she entered the kitchen with a bright smile on her face. But even her cheerful greeting couldn't dispel the cloud of anxiety that hung over him.

Even as he poured himself a cup of coffee, his hand trembled uncontrollably, a familiar feeling of panic rising within him. Focusing on the present felt like an impossible task.

The feeling clung to him for the rest of the day. His anxiety whispered doubts and fears in his ears at every turn, but he hid it well. No one knew. No one could know.

And even as Mark went to bed that night, his worries were still his companions. He felt like a failure, his anxiety robbing him of the peace and happiness he desperately craved.

Anxiety is a common emotion that most people experience at one point or another in life. Anxiety can be mild and transient — for example, you can become anxious because you are starting a new job or meeting someone for the first time. Before becoming parents, most of us considered parenting our children a time of wonder, happiness, and satisfaction. I thought all I had to deal with was changing diapers and running a bath. Parenting is obviously a lot more than that, and that alone is more than enough to make one super anxious.

Having children means dealing with many stressors (as though there aren't enough of those already) — including hormonal changes, sleep deprivation, and additional responsibilities. It also means losing many of the freedoms you once had and the sense of being in control.

Many parents experience anxiety symptoms within the first few months of becoming parents. Up to 35% of parents experience anxiety during pregnancy, 17% shortly after giving birth, and 20% six weeks later (Nakić 2018). However, parental anxiety does not necessarily end after the newborn period ends. The pandemic also added stress components to the mix such as the fear of your family getting sick and the anxiety of balancing work with children.

A study from 2020 found that more than 44% of parents experienced clinical anxiety related to the stress of the pandemic (A.L. van 2020). So, how do you deal with anxiety as a parent? Read on to find out.

Recognizing Anxiety Patterns in Parenting

Anxiety is normal, but it can be quite unnerving when it becomes a pattern, and when that happens, you have to recognize and address it. There are different types of anxiety disorders; some of the most common among parents include Generalized Anxiety Disorder (GAD), Social Anxiety Disorder (SAD), Panic Disorder, and Obsessive-Compulsive Disorder (OCD).

Those who have GAD constantly worry about various aspects of their lives, including their children's health, safety, finances, and work. This worry can be overwhelming and persistent, making it difficult to live in the present with the constant buzz of thoughts in your head.

SAD is more of the fear of social situations and interacting with others. That means you worry about what everyone thinks about you such as other parents, caregivers, and your kid's teachers. This fear can lead you to avoid social activities, greatly impacting your child's social experiences. Imagine canceling your child's soccer games because you get anxious around groups of people.

Panic Disorder involves sudden and unexpected panic attacks, which can be terrifying. These attacks often come with physical symptoms like chest pain, shortness of breath, and dizziness. If you've ever experienced these symptoms, you should see a doctor: If left untreated, this disorder can degenerate into something else and even traumatize your kids.

OCD is characterized by intrusive thoughts (obsessions) and repetitive behaviors (compulsions). You might constantly worry about your children's safety or health and want to repeatedly check on and clean up after them. As good as these activities are, they can be time- and energy-consuming when you overdo them.

Anxiety can manifest in various ways, both physically and emotionally. Physically, you could feel chest pain, shortness of breath, dizziness, sweating, trembling, muscle tension, headaches, stomachaches, or difficulty sleeping, all of which can take a toll on your health. Emotionally, anxiety often brings about worry, fear, irritability, restlessness, difficulty concentrating, and feeling overwhelmed. Behaviorally, anxiety can lead to avoidance behaviors. Those with anxiety might just want to avoid every possible social situation, which might mean they miss out on essential family activities. This, in turn, can lead to repetitive behaviors like excessive checking or cleaning (OCD). These behaviors can hinder your child's development and limit your ability to create lasting memories together.

Mindful Breathing and Relaxation Techniques

We talked about mindfulness earlier, and mindful breathing is another step up the ladder. Just like mindfulness, mindful breathing focuses on your breath without judgment. You can do this anywhere, but finding a quiet, comfortable spot can help you get the most out of it. Start by closing your eyes and directing your attention to your breath. Stay in the moment and feel the gentle rise and fall of your chest or the expansion and contraction of your stomach as you breathe in and out. It's okay if your thoughts wander; just gently guide yourself consciously back to your breath.

For relaxation techniques, there are methods to reduce muscle tension and promote calmness. Common relaxation techniques include deep breathing, progressive muscle relaxation, and guided imagery. Deep breathing is as simple as it sounds. Take slow, deep breaths through your nose, allowing your stomach to expand as you inhale, and then exhale slowly through your mouth. This process can calm your nerves and help you regain your composure.

Progressive muscle relaxation involves systematically tensing and relaxing different muscle groups in your body, one at a time, starting from your toes and working up to your head. It's like giving your body a reset button that can help you release built-up tension and stress.

Integrating mindful breathing and relaxation techniques into your daily routine can be beneficial. Beyond temporary relief, mindful breathing and relaxation techniques can profoundly change your overall well-being over time. These techniques are good at helping you reduce stress and anxiety. Imagine being able to dial down the racing thoughts and worries that often accompany parenting. Soothing, right? Mindful breathing and relaxation techniques will help you do just that. I like to think of them as a cool cup of water on a hot day.

They can also help improve your mood and emotional regulation. As I explained earlier, emotional regulation can help you parent better, and mindful breathing and relaxation techniques help you with that. I remember when my son was a toddler, I barely slept at night. Even though he's grown up now, I still find it hard sometimes to get quality sleep. These practices can help promote better sleep patterns. When you can calm your mind and relax your body, you create better conditions for restful nights.

Mindful breathing and relaxation can also offer relief from physical pain or discomfort. Releasing muscle tension comes into play again as the exercises help you reduce the perception of pain, giving you a natural and non-invasive way to manage discomfort.

Now, here's a surprising bonus: These practices go beyond your emotional well-being; they can also make a big difference in your physical health. Beyond the physical and emotional benefits, these techniques can increase your self-awareness and, invariably, your empathy toward others. As you become more attuned to your thoughts and feelings, you get to know yourself better and learn to be present. This can help your relationship with your children and those around you.

If you're new to mindful breathing and relaxation techniques, there's no need to rush. Start small and gradually increase the time you spend practicing. To get you started, here's a straightforward mindful breathing exercise that you can practice at any time of the day. I find it particularly helpful in the morning to start my day with clarity or at night to unwind before sleep.

1. Find a quiet, comfortable place to sit or lie down.
2. Close your eyes and place one hand on your chest and the other on your stomach.
3. Take a slow, deep breath through your nose, feeling your stomach rise as you inhale.
4. Exhale slowly through your mouth, noticing your stomach contracting as you exhale.
5. Continue to breathe this way for 5-10 minutes.
6. If your mind wanders, gently redirect your focus to your breath.
7. When you're finished, take a few deep breaths and slowly open your eyes.

Grounding Exercises for Anxiety

Grounding exercises can help you loosen up when anxiety puts a grip on you. You need your senses and a willingness to stay in the present moment. Consider these the antidote to racing thoughts and turbulent emotions.

Let's start with physical grounding techniques that harness your five senses and tangible objects to help you overcome anxiety. I made a list of simple, effective exercises below:

1. **Put your hands in water**: Find a container of water and put your hands in it. Pay close attention to the temperature and the sensations on your fingertips, palms, and the backs of your

hands. Does it feel the same across all areas? Experiment with warm water followed by cold, and then reverse. Notice how the transition from cold to warm differs from that of warm to cold.

2. **Breathe deeply**: Inhale slowly and deeply, then exhale with the same deliberate pace. You can even say or think "in" and "out" with each breath, feel the air fill your lungs, and then release it.

3. **Savor a food or drink**: Take small, deliberate bites or sips of something you enjoy. Allow yourself to fully taste and savor each morsel. Pay attention to the flavors, textures, and smells, relishing the sensations that linger on your tongue.

4. **Take a short walk**: Walk a few steps, concentrating on your footsteps. You can even count them if it helps. Feel the rhythm of your steps, the connection with the ground as your foot touches and lifts off, and the gentle sway of your body in motion.

5. **Hold a piece of ice**: Grab a piece of ice and observe its initial sensation. How does it feel on your skin? Note how it changes as it begins to melt and the sensation shifts.

6. **Move your body**: Do some simple exercises or stretches, like jumping jacks, jogging in place, or stretching different muscle groups one by one.

7. **Listen to your surroundings**: Pause for a moment and absorb the sounds around you. Are birds singing, dogs barking, machines humming, or is traffic buzzing? If people are talking, can you discern their conversations? Let these sounds wash over you, grounding you in your environment.

8. **Feel your body**: Whether sitting or standing, shift your focus to your body. Notice how each part feels, from the weight of your shirt on your shoulders to the sensation of your heartbeat and whether your stomach is content or if you feel hungry. Curl your fingers, wiggle your toes, and pay attention to how the floor feels against your feet.

9. **Try the 5-4-3-2-1 method**: Start from 5 and work backward; begin with five things you hear, then four things you see, three things you can touch from your current position, two things you can smell, and finally, one thing you can taste. Dive into the details, noticing the nuances you might usually overlook.

Mental grounding techniques, on the other hand, employ mental distractions to redirect your thoughts away from distressing feelings and back to the here and now. Let me go into more detail.

10. **Think in categories**: Pick one or two broad categories like "musical instruments" or "ice cream flavors," list as many items from each category as you can within a minute or so.

11. **Use math and numbers**: Remember times tables? You can challenge your mind by running through times tables, counting backward from 100, or finding various ways to make a chosen number, like 17 (e.g., 6 + 11, 20 - 3, 8 × 2 + 1, and so on).

12. **Recite something**: Retrieve a poem, song, or book passage you know by heart and recite it quietly to yourself or in your head. If you speak the words aloud, focus on the shape of each word on your lips and in your mouth.

13. **Make yourself laugh**: Invent a silly joke or watch something that tickles your funny bone, whether it's a funny animal video, a comedian's performance, or a hilarious TV show moment.

14. **Use an anchoring statement**: Adopt a statement that firmly roots you in the present, including details about who you are, where you are, the date and time, and what you're doing. Add more specifics until you feel calm and anchored.

15. **Imagine leaving painful feelings behind**: Visualize gathering your distressing emotions and placing them in a box. Then, picture yourself walking, swimming, biking, or jogging away from these feelings. Alternatively, you can think of your distressing thoughts as a TV show or song you dislike and change the channel or lower the volume.

16. **Describe your surroundings**: Take a few minutes to closely observe your environment, using all five senses to provide as much detail as possible. Describe what you see, hear, feel, and even smell. This practice helps anchor you in the present.

These mental grounding techniques are like a switch that redirects your focus. Experiment with them, and over time, you'll discover which ones work best for you.

Before and after employing a grounding exercise, take a moment to rate your distress level on a scale from 1 to 10. This will help you gauge the effectiveness of each technique and make adjustments as needed.

Building Resilience: Emotional Regulation in Stressful Situations

If you really want to beat anxiety, you need to pay attention to building resilience and mastering emotional regulation. As a parent, it's important to develop these skills, not just for yourself but also for your children. One way to build resilience is to develop healthy coping mechanisms. These are your emotional toolbox and include techniques and activities that help you manage stress and anxiety. Engaging in regular exercise, practicing relaxation techniques like mindful breathing (which we discussed earlier), and spending quality time with loved ones are excellent ways to nurture your emotional well-being.

No one can go through life's challenges alone. You need a reliable support network: Surround yourself with friends, family, or even support groups where you can share your thoughts and feelings. Connecting with others who understand what you're going through can help you make headway during tough times.

One thing most parents overlook is self-care. Ensure you get enough sleep, maintain a balanced diet, and engage in regular physical activity (I cannot emphasize that enough). You can tackle anxiety better with a well-rested, healthy body. Taking care of your mental health is as important as your physical health.

Now, let me talk about some specific strategies for emotional regulation. One of the scientifically supported strategies for emotion regulation is reappraisal. This approach focuses on changing the way we think about and interpret situations that trigger negative emotions (Davis, Senghas, Brandt, & Ochsner 2010). Instead of trying to suppress or forcibly eliminate these emotions, reappraisal helps you to find better ways of dealing with them. It's about shifting our perspective and looking for more positive and constructive angles. When you do so, you not only reduce the impact of negative emotions but also promote long-term well-being. Think of it as a way to reframe challenging situations.

Self-soothing is another valuable strategy for managing emotions, particularly those related to anger, sadness, and distressing experiences (Heiy & Cheavens, 2014). This approach emphasizes self-compassion and kindness. When you self-soothe, you recognize that you're experiencing difficult emotions and then take steps to comfort and nurture yourself. You can practice various self-soothing exercises such as self-compassion, loving up on yourself, listening to calming music, and reminiscing about positive memories. These practices can help mitigate the toxic effects of negative emotions and provide relief.

Developing a Daily Calming Routine

Mornings can be tough, can't they? I know how it feels when the worries and stress of the day ahead start piling up in your mind even before you've left your bed. It's like a weight in your stomach that makes you want to stay under the covers a little longer. But, interestingly, avoiding these feelings only makes them grow. What can help, however, is quite the opposite: Getting up a bit earlier and dedicating time to a morning routine. These days, my routine includes making a refreshing iced coffee, taking my dog for a walk, doing a quick workout, jotting down my to-do list, and, when time allows, meditating and journaling.

A morning filled with worries often leads to an anxious afternoon. On the contrary, starting your day with intention and calmness can make everything else feel more manageable. So, how can you create morning rituals that calm your racing mind, and most importantly, stick with them?

First, be realistic about how much time you can dedicate. We have different schedules and responsibilities, so determine what works for you. Whether it's an hour or just 20 minutes, find a time frame you can consistently work with. Don't sacrifice a good night's sleep to become an early riser; sleep helps your emotional regulation, and lack of it can leave you pretty grumpy.

Experiment to figure out which morning rituals work best for you. What works for someone else might not be the right fit for you. Make your morning routine enjoyable and easy to integrate into your life. You don't need an elaborate 20-step process; sometimes, small, positive changes you enjoy are all you need. Preparing a few things the night before, like your workout clothes or breakfast, can make your morning smoother. Let me share some habits that have helped me develop a calming morning routine:

1. **Start Your Day with Water:** As soon as you wake up, drink a glass of water before reaching for your tea or coffee. This simple act can boost your cognitive function, mood, energy, and emotional regulation. Plus, it's a great way to transition into the next part of your routine.

2. **Take a Morning Walk:** A morning stroll outdoors is a grounding way to begin your day. It exposes you to natural light, which can elevate your mood by stimulating serotonin.

3. **Avoid Checking Your Phone First Thing:** Resist the temptation to check work emails or social media as soon as you wake up. This can put you in "work mode" and trigger anxiety

before you even leave your bed. Try charging your phone across the room or outside your bedroom.

4. **Have a Good Breakfast:** Start with a balanced breakfast containing protein, healthy fats, fiber, and complex carbohydrates. Refined carbs like sugary cereals can lead to blood sugar spikes and crashes, affecting emotional regulation. Food should be enjoyed, so indulge occasionally, but don't overdo it: Prioritize good food over junk.

5. **Read a Few Pages from a Book:** Instead of checking the news or social media, pick up a book that inspires you and read, even if it's just a few pages.

To stick to your morning routine, set clear and specific goals. Avoid vague goals like "I want to work out in the morning." Instead, be concrete: "I'll do a workout at 7:30 a.m. after I finish my tea." Consistency is key. Get up around the same time every day and outline the activities you want to include in your routine and their order. Creating a habit makes your morning ritual feel automatic, relying less on your mood, motivation, or willpower. Each activity becomes a cue for the next; your morning routine will flow effortlessly with time. Just like when you take a shower, you shampoo, condition, shave, and wash your body in a specific order without much thought. Your morning routine can become easier when it is automatic because the routine is clear and you've created a habit.

Practical Worksheet: My Anxiety Coping Toolbox

Use your anxiety-coping toolbox whenever you feel anxious. You can also use your coping skills preventively, such as before you enter a situation that you know typically makes you anxious.

Step 1: Identify your coping skills

Think about all the ways you cope with anxiety. This can include relaxation techniques, cognitive-behavioral therapy (CBT) skills, or other strategies. Make a list of all of your coping skills.

Coping Skill	Description

Step 2: Choose your top coping skills

From your list, choose the top five or six you think are most helpful to you. These are the coping skills you will put in your anxiety coping toolbox.

Top Coping Skill	Description

Step 3: Write down your coping skills

Take a piece of paper and write down each of your top coping skills. Be sure to include instructions on how to use each one. For example, if you chose deep breathing, you might write:

Deep Breathing:

- Sit in a comfortable position and close your eyes.
- Place one hand on your chest and the other hand on your stomach.
- Breathe in slowly and deeply through your nose.
- Feel your stomach rise as you breathe in.
- Breathe out slowly through your mouth.
- Feel your stomach fall as you breathe out.
- Continue breathing deeply and slowly for five minutes.

1. _____
_____
_____
_____
_____
_____

2. _____
_____
_____
_____
_____
_____

3. _____

4. _____

_____

5. _____

Step 4: Decorate your anxiety coping toolbox

Once you have written down all of your coping skills, you can decorate your anxiety-coping toolbox. You can use markers, crayons, or other art supplies to make your toolbox look however you like.

Step 5: Keep your anxiety coping toolbox handy

Once your toolbox is complete, keep it in a place where you can easily access it. This could be on your nightstand, in your car, or in your purse or briefcase.

Takeaway Three

- As parents, you need to know that teaching emotional intelligence to your kids is just as important as academic skills. It lays the foundation for their personal and professional success by helping them effectively navigate relationships and challenges.
- Resilience, or the ability to bounce back from tough times, can be nurtured in your children. By encouraging them to face challenges, you help to build resilience and equip them with crucial life skills.
- Healthy coping mechanisms like exercise, relaxation, and social support can be very helpful in managing stress. Developing emotional regulation skills takes time and practice.
- Science-based strategies like reappraisal help manage emotions effectively. Self-soothing, exercises including meditation and reminiscence therapy, can reduce emotional distress. Attentional control involves diverting focus from negative emotions to positive perspectives.

CHAPTER FOUR

Anxiety Coping Skills for Kids (Ages 3-7)

"If you have good thoughts, they will shine out of your face like sunbeams, and you will always look lovely!"

— Roald Dahl

"The Lord is my strength and my shield; My heart trusted in Him, and I am helped."

— Psalms 28:7 (NKJV)

I remember reading a book to my kid when he was much younger titled "David and the Worry Beast." David was a young boy who was always worried. He worried about everything from getting sick to doing badly in school to playing poorly in soccer games. One day, David met a Worry Beast. The Worry Beast was a giant animal that fed on worries. David was initially scared of the Worry Beast, but he soon learned that the Worry Beast could help him manage his worries.

The Worry Beast taught David that it's okay to feel worried sometimes. Everyone worries from time to time, but if we let our worries control us, they can make our lives very difficult. The Worry Beast also taught David how to cope with his worries. He taught David to breathe deeply and to think about positive things. He also taught David to talk to his parents and other trusted adults about his worries.

With the Worry Beast's help, David learned to manage his worries and live a happier and more fulfilling life. The book ended with David and the Worry Beast becoming friends. David learned that he could always call on the Worry Beast for help if he ever felt overwhelmed by his worries.

The story was very helpful in teaching my son what worry means, and I also took the opportunity to teach him some life skills along that line. Just as you have learned how to cope with anxiety, your kid also needs to learn, and this chapter will provide you with all you need to teach them.

Understanding Childhood Anxiety

Case Study

Denise noticed that her daughter was picking at her dinner once again. She's been retreating to her room earlier than usual for the past few weeks. At first, Denise thought it was fatigue from school, especially since her daughter was no longer excited about going. But now with the lack of appetite, Denise sensed something deeper was troubling her child.

"Chloe, what's the matter?" she asked gently, for the fifth night in a row.

"Nothing," Chloe replied once again and forced a smile.

Denise wanted to ask more questions, but her husband touched her, signaling that she should let it be. He already told her Chloe would open up when she was ready the last time she expressed her concerns to him.

One morning, she found Chloe huddled in her bed, tears streaming down her cheeks, and refusing to go to school. When asked what happened, she hesitated before confessing about her overwhelming fears at school and making friends.

She had not been able to make a new friend since her best friend relocated, and she was scared of being rejected when she tried to make new ones. Denise's heart broke, seeing her child in anguish. She held Chloe close, assuring her that she wasn't alone.

As a parent, noticing behavior in your child that raises concern is common. Sometimes, you might sense something isn't quite right, even if you can't put your finger on it. Childhood anxiety can manifest in various ways, including avoidance of activities, irritability, and difficulties with sleep. These signs can be more than just typical childhood behavior.

Anxiety in children often stems from environmental stressors such as trauma, losing a loved one, school-related issues, or experiences with bullying. These factors, among others, can lead to anxiety-related problems. This combined effect can lead to social isolation and stigmatization and hinder their ability to be active community members.

Anxiety is the most prevalent mental health disorder, affecting countless young people in the United States. Anxiety disorders often manifest as excessive worry about daily events or activities, such as schoolwork or homework, to the point where it disrupts education, work, or social life.

How common is anxiety in young people? Research estimates that around 32% of adolescents in the United States experience an anxiety disorder (NIH 2020). While anxiety disorders affect females more often than males, age, ethnicity, and geography do not significantly determine who develops it. Unfortunately, only 7% of young people who need mental health support receive it despite the prevalence (WHO 2021).

Clinical anxiety goes beyond the everyday experience of stress and can interfere significantly with your child's daily life. Differentiating between various forms of anxiety including stress, fear, uncertainty, panic, and social anxiety, can help you understand your child's symptoms and select appropriate strategies for support.

- **Stress vs. Anxiety**: Stress typically arises from external triggers like taking an exam or conflicts with peers. Anxiety, in contrast, can originate internally and persist over time, even after the stressor has been removed.

- **Fear vs. Anxiety**: Fear is a response to a real or perceived threat, while anxiety is the anticipation of future threats. Sometimes, "anxiety" describes ongoing nervousness or persistent tension or worry.

- **Uncertainty**: Children with anxiety often struggle with uncertainty, viewing it as a precursor to adverse outcomes. This fear of the unknown can lead to avoidance behaviors, reinforcing anxiety over time.

- **Panic**: Panic attacks are intense surges of anxiety characterized by rapid heartbeat, sweating, chest pain, shortness of breath, dizziness, and stomach discomfort. Panic attacks can be triggered or seemingly come out of nowhere, and they differ from the more prolonged, gradual nature of anxiety.

Social Anxiety

Social anxiety disorder concerns the fear of being judged or embarrassed in social situations. For children, social anxiety often manifests in peer settings such as school or extracurricular activities, or when interacting with adults or authority figures. At its core, social anxiety in children and teens revolves around the fear of negative evaluation from others. They might worry about being perceived as anxious, weak, unintelligent, dull, intimidating, dirty, or unlikable. Some children even fear offending others and facing rejection as a consequence. Socially anxious children might avoid numerous social experiences such as class participation, eating in front of others, joining extracurricular activities, ordering in restaurants, using public restrooms, and attending social events with peers.

Separation Anxiety

Separation anxiety disorder is one of the most common anxiety disorders in children, and it typically peaks around age three. Children with separation anxiety worry that something terrible will happen to them or their caregivers upon separation. This anxiety can lead to excessive worrying, sleep problems, social difficulties, physical anxiety symptoms, or issues at school. While most children eventually outgrow separation anxiety as they mature and understand that separation is not permanent, those with separation anxiety disorder continue to experience these anxieties.

Phobias

Phobias involve intense fears of specific objects or situations that disrupt daily life. Common phobias in children and teens include hemophobia (fear of blood), emetophobia (fear of vomiting), and trypanophobia (fear of needles or medical procedures involving injections). Phobias are typically present for six months or longer and can significantly affect a person's quality of life.

Selective Mutism

Selective mutism manifests as a child's difficulty speaking in specific social settings such as at school or in public. Interestingly, these children can speak freely in other settings, like at home with family. Selective mutism is often rooted in anxiety, making it challenging for affected children to communicate outside their home environment.

Despite its common usage, anxiety remains widely misunderstood. Dispelling some common myths about anxiety can aid in better understanding the condition in children and teens.

- **Myth: People Can Just "Snap Out" of Being Anxious**: Anxiety doesn't work like a switch. The fears and worries of an anxious child or teen, even if they appear trivial, are authentic and not easily dismissed. Professional help is often needed to break the cycle of anxiety and avoidance.
- **Myth: Anxiety Isn't Treatable**: Anxiety is highly treatable. Each case of anxiety is unique, and what works for one person

might not work for another. Finding the proper treatment and support tailored to each child's need requires patience.

- **Myth: People Need Medication to Manage Their Anxiety**: Long-term medication use is not always necessary to treat anxiety. While short-term medication might initially be recommended to reduce symptoms, there are numerous successful evidence-based approaches to managing anxiety, including meditation, therapy, exercise, and more. Medication is just one option.

- **Myth: Kids Aren't Anxious, They're Just Shy**: Shyness and social anxiety differ. Shyness is a part of a child's personality, whereas social anxiety involves a fear of embarrassment in social situations that leads to avoidance.

- **Myth: Children and Teens Don't Have Anxiety, They're Just Looking for Attention.** Anxiety can manifest in various physical and behavioral symptoms such as anger, irritability, sleep disturbances, withdrawal, or tantrums. These behaviors can draw attention, but they often indicate underlying anxiety that must be addressed.

So, how do you know if your child has anxiety? Recognizing anxiety in children involves paying attention to physical and emotional or behavioral symptoms. Not every child will show all these signs. Still, you need to stay vigilant to identify potential issues:

Physical Symptoms of Anxiety:

- Consistent stomachaches or headaches

- Racing heart
- Shortness of breath
- Gastrointestinal issues including nausea and vomiting
- Irritability or easy agitation
- Sleep disturbances including frequent nightmares
- Low energy
- Restlessness or an inability to sit still
- Frequent tantrums

Emotional and Behavioral Symptoms of Anxiety:

- Repeatedly discussing fears and worries
- Spending more time alone or avoiding social events
- Deteriorating academic performance, including class avoidance or skipping school altogether

Several factors can contribute to anxiety, including genetic, learned, environmental, and biological influences.

- **Genetic**: Children can inherit a predisposition to anxiety from their parents, just as they might inherit physical traits like height.
- **Learned**: Children can also pick up anxious behaviors from their surroundings, including family members or caregivers who exhibit the trait. Caregivers modeling fear or avoidance of specific situations or objects can contribute to a child's anxiety.

- **Environmental**: Anxiety can develop following stressful events like the death of a loved one, illness, frequent relocations, bullying, or abuse. Additionally, anxiety can co-occur with other mental health conditions such as depression, attention-deficit/hyperactivity disorder, autism spectrum disorders, and eating disorders.
- **Biological**: Neurotransmitters in the brain are crucial in regulating emotions. When these neurotransmitters don't function correctly, a person can be biologically predisposed to anxiety.

Anxiety disorders are treatable, and various approaches can be effective in helping you manage your kid's anxiety.

- **Therapy**: Most treatments for anxiety involve talk therapy or psychotherapy. Cognitive-behavioral therapy (CBT) with exposure and response prevention therapy (ERP), acceptance and commitment therapy (ACT), and interpersonal therapy (IPT) are standard evidence-based therapies for pediatric anxiety. These therapies help patients identify and change negative thought patterns, develop coping strategies, and manage their symptoms effectively.
- **Medication**: While not always necessary, doctors can prescribe medication for anxiety. Selective serotonin reuptake inhibitors (SSRIs) are a class of medication that can help alleviate anxiety and its often co-occurring symptoms of depression.

Child-Friendly Mindfulness Practices

Young minds are naturally curious about their bodies, and it's an ideal age to instill body-mind awareness as self-care. Mindfulness can be a playful experience for kids, and one enjoyable entry point is through body poses. Explain to your children that these fun poses can help them feel strong, brave, and happy. Then, encourage them to try one of these engaging poses:

1. **The Superman**: Stand with your feet just a bit wider than your hips, clench your fists, and reach your arms toward the sky, stretching your body as tall as possible.

2. **The Wonder Woman**: Stand tall with your legs wider than hip-width apart and place your hands or fists on your hips.

Ask your kids how they feel after a few rounds of practicing these poses. You might be pleasantly surprised by their responses.

Spidey Senses

Drawing inspiration from superheroes, you can teach kids how to stay present by activating their "Spidey senses." Like Spider-Man's super-focused abilities, these senses encompass smell, sight, hearing, taste, and touch. You can teach children to turn on their Spidey senses to observe and appreciate the world around them. This exercise cultivates mindfulness by urging them to pause and focus on the present moment.

The Mindful Jar

This engaging activity is a powerful way to help children understand how strong emotions can overwhelm them and how to find calmness amid such emotions.

To get started, you'll need a clear jar (like a Mason jar) filled almost to the top with water. Add a generous spoonful of glitter glue or dry glitter to the jar and seal it with the lid. Shake the jar to make the glitter swirl.

Use this script or create your mini-lesson:

"Imagine that the glitter represents your thoughts when you're stressed, angry, or upset. Notice how they swirl around, making it challenging to see clearly? This is why it's easy to make hasty decisions when you're upset—your thoughts become cloudy. But remember, this is normal; it happens to all of us, even grown-ups.

[Place the jar in front of them.]

Now, watch what happens when you stay still for a few moments. Keep watching. Notice how the glitter starts to settle, and the water becomes clear. Your mind functions similarly. When you stay calm, your thoughts settle, and you gain a clearer perspective. Taking deep breaths during this calming process can help us find clarity when we're overwhelmed by emotions."

This exercise helps children recognize the impact of emotions on their thoughts and introduces mindfulness by focusing on the swirling glitter in the jar. You can also encourage them to focus on one emotion at a time, such as anger, and discuss how the swirling versus settling glitter parallels that emotion.

Safari

The safari exercise transforms an ordinary walk into an exciting adventure for your children. Explain to them that you're embarking on a safari, and their mission is to spot as many birds, bugs, creepy crawlies, and other creatures as possible. Anything that walks, crawls, swims, or flies is fair game. To succeed, they must engage all their senses, especially the little ones.

This activity turns an everyday walk into a thrilling quest for discovery. Much like a mindful walk does for adults, this exercise fosters awareness and grounding in the present for children.

Incorporating these child-friendly mindfulness practices into your child's daily routine can help them develop valuable skills for managing their emotions, staying present, and nurturing their overall well-being.

You need to approach your child with purpose and positivity to get your child to practice mindfulness. This is not a disciplinary tool but a life skill that can benefit their emotional well-being. Keep in mind the true purpose of mindfulness practice. Use it as a tool to promote positivity and emotional growth rather than a form of punishment or discipline. Children are more likely to engage in mindfulness when they can associate it with positive experiences.

Creative Expression for Anxiety Relief

Creative expression can help you and your child manage anxiety. It's a process that allows you to express your thoughts, feelings, and experiences through various creative activities. Whether drawing, playing music, writing, moving, or immersing in nature, these activities can help relieve anxiety for children and adults.

Creative activities can be a welcome distraction from anxious thoughts and help release built-up stress, making relaxing easier. Creative expression promotes self-awareness and understanding. These activities help your child to better relate to their emotions and experiences. They also have a particular way of promoting relaxation and well-being.

Drawing, painting, sculpting, and other artistic endeavors are excellent ways to express emotions and experiences. You can try art therapy, a specialized form of art that uses art to deal with anxiety. You can also try music. Whether playing an instrument, singing, or simply listening to music, its power to calm and relax is remarkable. I introduced my son to classical music when he was younger, and now I think he loves it more than I do.

Writing in a journal, composing poetry, or writing stories can also help your kids process thoughts and emotions. It also helps to combat negative thought patterns and build coping skills. It's also an excellent way to introduce your child to creative writing. Spending quality time in nature, gardening, hiking, or simply appreciating the outdoors can be calming. Nature has a unique ability to reduce stress and enhance mood.

Finding the creative activities that work best for your child might take some time. Be patient and allow them to explore various options. There's no right or wrong way to engage in creative activities.

The Power of Play: Games to Manage Anxiety

I want you to understand games' potential in helping your child manage anxiety. These are not just games; they are tools that can offer your child comfort, help them build strength, and create opportunities for valuable conversations. I'll discuss four games I've found helpful: Jenga, Don't Break the Ice, Hedbanz, and Race to the Treasure. Additionally, I'll introduce you to a simple yet effective activity involving bubbles.

Let's begin with Jenga. At first glance, it's a tower of wooden blocks, but it's much more than that. It's a way to work through the complex emotions that often follow decision-making and the fear of failure.

When your child selects a block, they are making a choice, and this opens the door to discussing the feelings surrounding choices — the excitement, the fear of choosing the wrong one, and the anticipation of what might happen next.

To set up a game of Jenga, you'll need to stack the blocks in three groups to build a tower. Shake the Jenga blocks out of the box onto a flat surface, then stack the blocks in parallel sets of three until you have an 18-block-high tower. Ensure the structure is sturdy and that each block layer interlocks to make the tower stand tall without external support.

There's no limit on the number of players; it can even be played solo. For a competitive game, find at least one other player and have everyone sit in a circle around the block structure. About 4-6 players is an excellent range to ensure everyone can participate without waiting too long for their turn.

Consider writing questions or dares on the blocks before stacking them to add a twist to the game. This optional variation makes each block pull more exciting; questions can range from thoughtful or humorous and dares can be anything from reciting the multiplication table to acting like a cartoon character.

Next, designate a player to make the first block pull. Traditionally, it's the person who built the tower, but you can choose based on birthdays or a simple game of Rock, Paper, Scissors. Removing a block without toppling the tower requires patience and steady hands. Players can only touch the tower one hand at a time to make it more challenging.

Each pulled block should be placed atop the tower, perpendicular to the last row, continuing the layering pattern in groups of three. As the game progresses, the tower will grow taller, becoming more precarious. The game continues until the tower falls, and the last person to successfully place a block on top wins. Regardless of the outcome, always remember to rebuild the tower and play again.

Emphasize the importance of patience and moving slowly in Jenga. Rushing can lead to the tower being toppled prematurely. If a block doesn't seem loose, avoid forcing it; it might loosen up later. When searching for easy blocks, gently test each by poking the tower. Take blocks from the top or middle of the stack, as the bottom ones are often difficult to remove.

Use just one or two fingers to push or pull the blocks, making as little contact with the tower as possible. When placing blocks, consider how the tower tilts after removing and arranging your block to balance it. This tactic can make it harder for the next player to pull a block and maintain the tower's stability.

Jenga teaches your child valuable life lessons about making choices and handling setbacks. It is also an excellent tool for discussing these concepts while having fun with friends and family.

Moving on to "Don't Break the Ice." This children's board game is designed for one or more players to be the last player standing without dropping the plastic animal. Place the ice tray upside down to set up the game, allowing players to insert the ice blocks into the tray. Start by placing the giant ice block centrally, surrounded by the remaining blocks, pressed tightly together to ensure they hold up when the tray is turned over. Finally, position the plastic animal on the large ice block.

The gameplay in "Don't Break the Ice" is straightforward. The first player, chosen randomly or as the youngest, starts the game. Play proceeds clockwise, with each player taking a turn using a hammer to hit an ice block. The goal is to dislodge the chosen ice block from the tray without causing the plastic animal or the large block to fall. Once players select an ice block, they cannot change their minds, even if other blocks fall while hammering away at their choice. The game ends when the plastic animal and large block fall out of the tray, or when playing with multiple players, the player who dislodged the animal is eliminated, and rounds continue until one player remains.

In this game, every turn your child takes and every ice block they select involves making choices. These choices might go as planned or not, just like in everyday life. "Don't Break the Ice" is an excellent conversation starter about decision-making and the possibility of things not going as expected. It's an opportunity to discuss recovery, bouncing back when things don't go your way, and the importance of perseverance.

The game fosters a sense of responsibility for one's choices and teaches that sometimes, you must adapt and continue when faced with unexpected challenges. "Don't Break the Ice" encourages patience and strategy in a fun and engaging way.

Up next is "Hedbanz." This game is about guessing what object is depicted on the picture card attached to the players' headbands by asking yes-or-no questions. To set up "Hedbanz," separate the picture cards from the sample question cards and shuffle them. Place them face down in the center of the play area. Also, put the badges and sample question cards in the middle of the table within easy reach. Each player wears a headband, ensuring the Hedbanz logo is between their eyebrows. Players are given a picture card face-down to start with, and they insert it into the clip provided on the headband with the picture side showing.

The youngest player goes first. On their turn, they flip over the timer and start asking each of the other players "yes" or "no" questions to help identify the object on their card. Imagine a player has a card with a squirrel picture. They might start by asking, "Am I an animal?" If they receive a "yes" response, it guides them in the right direction. Subsequent questions could be, "Do I live on land?" or "Am I big or small?" or "Do I have fur?" Players continue asking questions, gathering information from other players to narrow their guesses.

Notably, the other players should not deliberately mislead the guesser. If the player cannot guess the object before the timer runs out, the picture remains on the headband, and play moves on to the next player. On their next turn, they continue asking questions about the unresolved card. If a player feels they are not close to guessing the object, they can decide to change the card on their next turn, and play continues.

Scoring in "Hedbanz" involves earning points for every badge attached to the headband. The first to collect three badges wins the game. Rounds do not have a predetermined number; the game ends when a player acquires three badges, earning three points and claiming victory. What makes "Hedbanz" unique is its cooperative nature. Instead of competing against each other, players work together toward a common goal: figuring out the object on their headband. This cooperative element builds healthy dialogue, encourages teamwork, and emphasizes that success can sometimes take time and effort.

"Race to the Treasure" is reminiscent of classic board games and offers a cooperative experience where players work together. Setting up "Race to the Treasure" involves dividing the board into a grid with letters A through F along the top and numbers 1 through 6 down the side. The board setup is dynamic, as you roll the letter and number dice to place keys and an ogre snack on the board. Next, shuffle ogre and path tiles into a pile or place them face-down in the box lid, which can prevent cards from scattering. Each player takes turns drawing tiles and placing them on the board. Pathway tiles come in various patterns, such as straight, L-turn, and T-intersection. When laying these tiles, players must align them to create open paths.

"Race to the Treasure" aims to collect three keys by placing path tiles on their corresponding critical locations along the board's bottom edge. Once three keys are collected, players race to reach the "end" square before the ogre does. Multiple paths can be followed, providing flexibility in gameplay.

Additionally, an ogre snack can be obtained in the same way as a key. Once acquired, the ogre snack can remove an ogre tile from the ogre track, eliminating a threat. The game ends when players successfully collect three keys and reach the "end" square or when enough ogre tiles are revealed to cause the ogre to reach the "end" space first.

Unlike other games, "Race to the Treasure" promotes cooperation and teamwork. Instead of trying to outdo each other, everyone collaborates toward a shared objective. This game encourages healthy communication and cooperation, making it especially valuable for anxious children. Through "Race to the Treasure," your child can learn the power of working together, the value of listening to others, and the joy of achieving a shared goal.

Finally, let's touch on blowing bubbles. While it might appear as child's play, it has a profound calming effect on the nervous system and the brain. To start, store a mixture of soap and water in a container. Get your child to blow bubbles using a bubble blower. You can make it more exciting by having them lie on their back as you blow bubbles over their head, watching as the bubbles gently float to the ground.

As your child takes deep breaths to blow the bubbles, their nervous system gradually calms. It's a simple yet effective way to help your child relax when anxiety strikes, teaching them that sometimes, it takes a moment of mindful play to find peace within.

Incorporating these games and activities into your child's routine can significantly affect their anxiety management. Each one offers unique opportunities for learning, growth, and connection. So, don't underestimate the power of play in helping your child thrive in the face of anxiety.

Gradual Exposure Techniques for Kids

Exposure Therapy might sound counterintuitive. Still, the concept is simple: gradually exposing children to the things that trigger their anxiety can teach them that these fears are manageable. Avoiding these triggers might provide temporary relief, but it doesn't address the root of the problem. Instead, exposure therapy helps your child understand that they can face their fears and be safe.

One of the most effective ways to help your child through anxiety is by sharing your experiences. I talked about this earlier, but I'll bring it back again. If you've dealt with anxiety in the past or are currently living with it, talking about your journey can help your child feel less alone and more understood. They need to know that anxiety is a common human experience and that it's okay to discuss it openly. By discussing your experiences with anxiety, you can normalize the conversation and show them it's possible to conquer their fears.

Books can be powerful tools to explain complex concepts like exposure therapy to children. Consider reading those that address anxiety and the process of gradually facing fears. Pause during the story to discuss how exposure works, emphasizing the difference between avoidance and exposure. For example, you can point out that when the book's character, Tommy, starts looking at pictures of dogs, he gradually realizes that he isn't in danger, which helps reduce his anxiety. Draw parallels between this process and other activities your child has learned, such as riding a bike without training wheels.

Children learn best when they're actively engaged. Ask your child questions throughout the book or have conversations about exposure to encourage their participation. For instance, inquire about Tommy's feelings during different tasks, asking questions like, "What do you think Tommy is feeling?" As Tommy progresses and his anxiety lessens, prompt your child to reflect on why Tommy's anxiety is decreasing. This helps your child understand the process and reinforces that confronting fears can reduce anxiety.

Creating a list of exposure tasks tailored to your child's fears is a collaborative effort. Start by having your child identify the things that make them most anxious or scare them the most, something they'd rate a ten on a fear scale of 1-10. Then, ask them to name something about their fear that frightens them less, perhaps rating it as a 1 or 2 on the scale. These benchmarks serve as starting points and endpoints, with a series of steps between to gradually expose your child to their fear. Each step should be repeated until it causes minimal or no anxiety, helping your child gain practice and confidence.

Your child needs you. Your presence and support are invaluable throughout the exposure therapy process. Exposure techniques can be stressful and trigger anticipatory anxiety, which occurs when someone waits for something to happen. When you actively support and encourage your child during exposure tasks, you can reduce their stress levels and make it more likely for them to stick with the process until they succeed.

It's natural to want to protect your children from distress. However, when it comes to exposure therapy, helping your child avoid their fears is counterproductive. It's important not to inadvertently enable avoidance behaviors. Encourage your child to confront their fears, providing guidance and reassurance as needed, but avoid the temptation to shield them from the source of their anxiety.

If your child's anxiety affects their daily life, it might be time to seek professional help. Don't hesitate to consult your child's primary care physician for guidance and referrals if required. Sometimes, the expertise of a mental health professional can make a world of difference in effectively guiding your child through exposure therapy.

Now that we've explored how to approach exposure therapy with your child, let's address something else: making the process engaging and enjoyable. Exposure therapy isn't always easy or fun, but adding an element of enjoyment can make it more manageable. Here are some creative ideas to engage your child in exposure therapy:

Turn It into a Game Show:

Create a playful atmosphere where completing exposures feels like winning a game. Don't hesitate to participate: Leading by example can be highly effective.

Replace OCD Rituals with Silly Movements:

If your child has physical rituals related to their anxiety, replace them with silly body movements. For example, have your child dance to a sidewalk crack instead of avoiding it. Instead of tapping on a table, do a fun fist bump with them.

Use Fun Materials for Contamination Exposures:

If contamination is a concern, incorporate enjoyable materials like paint, slime, sand, mud, oil, or glue into exposure activities. Engaging with these materials can make the process less intimidating.

Mess Up Appearances Together:

Have a session where everyone deliberately messes up something about their appearance. Encourage your child to put makeup on one eye, smear lipstick, create wild hairstyles, or intentionally miss a button on a shirt. This playful approach can help reduce the anxiety associated with perfectionism.

Challenge the Idea of Being "Wrong":

Challenge the fear of being wrong by purposely answering questions incorrectly or telling stories with exaggerated, incorrect details. For example, read a problematic tongue twister as fast as possible, prioritizing speed over accuracy.

Organize a Contamination Scavenger Hunt:

Walk around your neighborhood with your child and have them touch various triggering objects. This scavenger hunt encourages exposure to feared contaminants.

Trivia for Psycho-Education:

Engage your child in a trivia game that educates them about OCD-related concepts. Define terms like OCD, habituation, natural exposure, and planned exposure. Encourage discussions about overcoming OCD fears and differentiate between rituals and coping skills.

Play Act as OCD:

Role-play with your child, with you playing the part of their OCD (acting as the Worry Voice, Worry Trick, or False Alarm) while your child plays. This allows them to practice resisting the demands of their OCD.

"Make Wishes" Activity:

If your child worries that their thoughts can make bad things happen, engage them in a "make wishes" activity. Have them make wishes, like wishing you would win the lottery or for passing cars to get flat tires. This exercise challenges irrational beliefs about thought control.

Incorporate Art into Therapy:

Art can be a powerful medium for therapy. Help your child design a "fear thermometer" to gauge their anxiety levels. Encourage them to draw what OCD looks like to them. Have them draw preferred characters from Disney, Pokémon, or comics for added exposure and intentionally "mess them up." You can also work with wet clay or finger paint.

Let Your Child Be the Therapist:

Allow your child to take on the therapist's role and guide others on how to combat their OCD urges. This role reversal empowers them and reinforces their understanding of exposure therapy techniques.

Do Something "Bad" for Scrupulosity Fears:

If scrupulosity is a concern, engage in activities that challenge the fear of doing something "bad." Toilet paper the halls of your clinic, write something unconventional in a therapist's book, or temporarily say something that contradicts moral values.

Introduce Reinforcers and Rewards:

Motivate your child by offering reinforcers or rewards after each successful exposure task. It could be as simple as allowing them to choose a song from iTunes or Spotify in your office.

As you implement these engaging exposure techniques, closely observe your child's progress. Keep an eye out for the development of new habits and gradually reduce the "fun" aspect of exposures as your child becomes more adept at managing their anxiety. Remember that the goal is for them to experience discomfort and challenge themselves progressively, ultimately leading to reduced anxiety and improved coping skills.

Practical Worksheet: My Child's Anxiety Coping Plan

The Worry Tree

Let's start by creating a Worry Tree. This tree will help your child share and conquer their worries.

1. Print out the tree and apple templates provided below.

1. Find a cozy spot where you and your child can chat.
2. Ask your child about anything that's been bothering them lately. Have them write their worries on one of the apple cutouts if comfortable. If not, you can write it down for them.

3. Use a tack or adhesive to attach the apple to the tree. Explain that this tree is a safe place where worries can disappear and that there's no need to fret anymore.

4. If your child has more concerns, repeat the process by writing them on separate apples and sticking them to the tree.

2. Worry Journal Adventure

Steps	Instructions	Completed
1. Get a Journal	Get a special notebook or colorful sheets for the journal.	[ ]
2. Express Worries:	Encourage your child to write, draw, or create comics about worries.	[ ]
3. Rate Worries:	Have them rate worries from 1 to 10 (1 = tiny worry, 10 = giant worry).	[ ]
4. Share Thoughts:	Write down thoughts and feelings about each worry.	[ ]
5. Explore Together	Explore the journal together from time to time.	[ ]

3. Affirmations

1. Create a list of positive affirmations like, "I am strong," "I can handle anything," or, "I am a worry-busting hero."

2. Let your child choose their favorite affirmations.

3. Encourage them to repeat these affirmations every day, especially when they need a boost of confidence or when worries try to sneak in.

List some of these affirmations.

_____
_____
_____
_____
_____
_____

Takeaway Four

- As a parent, it's common to notice behavior in your child that raises concerns. Sometimes, you might sense that something isn't quite right, even if you can't put your finger on it.
- Childhood anxiety can manifest in various ways, including avoidance of activities, irritability, and difficulties with sleep. These signs can be more than just typical childhood behavior.
- Young minds are naturally curious about their bodies, and it's an ideal age to instill body-mind awareness as self-care. Mindfulness can be a playful experience for kids, and one enjoyable entry point is through body poses. Explain to your children that these fun poses can help them feel strong, brave, and happy.
- One of the most effective ways to help your child through anxiety is by sharing your experiences. If you've dealt with anxiety in the past or experience it currently, talking about your journey can help your child feel less alone and more understood.

- They need to know that anxiety is a common human experience, and it's okay to discuss it openly. By discussing your experiences with anxiety, you can normalize the conversation and show them that it's possible to conquer fears.

- Incorporating games and activities into your child's routine can significantly affect their anxiety management. Each one offers unique opportunities for learning, growth, and connection. Don't underestimate the power of play in helping your child thrive in the face of anxiety.

Your Review Can Help Unlock the Journey of Parenthood!

Hey Super Reader!

Wow, you've made it this far into our book! 💥 We're super thankful you're on this adventure of parenting with us. What you've learned could be a game-changer for lots of moms and dads out there.

Could you do us a big favor and share your thoughts on Amazon? Your honest words could be just the superhero cape another parent needs to fly through their day. 👩 👨 Imagine helping someone feel a little less alone and a lot more hopeful with just a few clicks.

It's super quick, we promise! Just 60 seconds of your time could sprinkle some extra happiness on families for years to come.

Thanks a million for your time and for sharing your superpowers.

Here's where you can leave your review.

Big high-fives and thank-yous,

Your Friends on This Crazy, Fun Parenting Journey,

The Team at SpreadLife Publishing

📖 Leave a review on Amazon US 📖

📖 Leave a review on Amazon UK 📖

CHAPTER FIVE
Modeling Emotional Regulation

"Teach children how they should live, and they will remember it all their life."

— Proverbs 22:6 (GNT)

I've always wondered how children learn to talk. One minute, they struggle to babble "Dada" and "Mama"; the next, they ask for a cup of water. Children are like sponges, soaking up everything around them. Just as they learn to talk by imitating and interacting, they also learn how to manage their emotions by observing and emulating. They learn emotional regulation by watching. If you react to anger with shouting and frustration, your kids will likely do the same. Conversely, if you demonstrate calmness and composure, they'll be more inclined to better handle their emotions.

Keep in mind that learning emotional regulation takes time. Just as your children need time to say their first words and form sentences, they'll also need time in this regard. Encourage their efforts, celebrate their progress, and be there to comfort them when they stumble along the way.

Understanding Emotional Regulation in Kids Aged 3-7

Case Study

As the day unfolded, tension rose in the Jones household. This wasn't Tiffany's first rodeo: Her two kids were always bickering and fighting, and she often ended up shouting at them to keep quiet. Even this time, she was starting to get annoyed. But her friend Sarah advised her to handle things a little differently, and she was going to try that out.

But first, deep breaths. She inhaled to a count of 5, held her breath for 5 counts, and exhaled for 5 counts. She kept doing this until she felt calm.

Then she calmly called both kids over and gently explained why they needed to understand each other's feelings and find common ground. She told them that it was okay to be angry or upset, it was what they did that mattered, and that taking a moment to breathe before reacting could prevent hurt feelings. Then, she showed them how to take mindful breaths and watched them practice.

After weeks of practicing this, Tiffany could boast of a calm family who took deep breaths instead of reacting and expressed themselves in calm words instead of raised voices.

All humans are born with emotions, but not all emotions are hardwired into our brains from birth. Children begin life with basic emotional reactions like crying, frustration, hunger, and pain. They gradually learn about more complex emotions as they grow.

While there is no universal consensus on which emotions are innate and which are learned, it is widely accepted that there are eight primary hardwired emotions: anger, sadness, fear, joy, interest, surprise, disgust, and shame. These primary emotions serve as the foundation for more complex emotional responses.

Secondary emotions, on the other hand, are linked to these primary emotions and develop due to a child's experiences. For example, if a child has experienced punishment during an emotional meltdown, they might feel anxiety the next time they become angry. These emotional layers can help you know how to support your child's emotional development.

How you react to your child's emotions can make or mar their emotional intelligence. Emotional invalidation, such as dismissing or ignoring a child's feelings, can hinder their ability to effectively manage emotions. On the other hand, when you help children identify and express their emotions, you help them express their feelings in socially appropriate ways.

Children's emotional experiences evolve as they age, and different age groups require varying forms of support. Infants rely heavily on pre-wired emotional responses during the first months of life. They cry to signal discomfort or seek pleasurable stimuli like food and physical contact. Research suggests that infants as young as six months can use self-soothing behaviors such as thumb-sucking, to manage distress (Henderson *et al.,* 2019*)*.

As a parent, you can help soothe your infant's emotions. Studies show that listening to songs can help maintain infant contentment for extended periods (Melanie *et al.*, 2011). Multimodal singing, such as

"The Wheels on the Bus," is more effective than lullabies in reducing distress.

When children reach their first birthday, they understand that parents can help them regulate their emotions. Toddlers become more aware of specific emotions associated with situations, with fear often being the most challenging. As a toddler parent, you can employ strategies like situation selection, modification, and distraction to help your child cope with anger and fear. Avoiding distressing situations and providing age-appropriate methods for handling emotions are effective ways to guide them during this developmental stage.

Children experience a wide range of emotions during childhood, including secondary ones influenced by their previous experiences. They become more capable of understanding appropriate emotional expressions but might struggle to identify and name their feelings.

To help children in this age group develop emotional regulation skills, focus on three key phases: helping them identify emotions, teaching them to recognize emotional triggers, and providing self-regulation strategies. Encourage open conversations about emotions, validate their feelings, and model appropriate emotional responses.

Your role as a parent is important in creating a safe and supportive environment where your child feels free to express their emotions. Secure children are more likely to develop and use effective emotion regulation skills to manage challenging feelings.

Emotional regulation is not a skill we are born with; it is a learned ability that profoundly impacts a child's life. Poor emotional regulation can lead to frequent tantrums, strained parent-child relationships, and difficulty forming and maintaining friendships. In contrast, strong emotional regulation skills contribute to improved relationships, academic success, and overall well-being.

Furthermore, children with effective emotional regulation skills are better equipped to handle adversity and are more resilient when facing trauma or difficult life events. On the other hand, poor emotional regulation is linked to various behavioral and emotional disorders, including Oppositional Defiant Disorder, anxiety disorders, eating disorders, and clinical depression.

Both genetics and their environment influence children's ability to regulate their emotions. While some babies might be temperamentally more predisposed to self-regulation, a parent's nurturing environment builds emotional development.

The brain's development in early childhood is more like building a house, where genetics provide the blueprint but life experiences act as the building materials. Early experiences significantly impact a child's emotional regulation abilities, and sensitive periods during development play a role in acquiring these skills.

Research has shown that children adopted into nurturing environments before age two can develop emotional regulation skills comparable to those who have never been institutionalized (Putnam *et al.,* 2015). This suggests that the sensitive period for emotional self-regulation is before age two, emphasizing the importance of early childhood experiences.

However, it's essential to note that even if a child has passed this sensitive period, it is never too late to start teaching emotional regulation skills. The process might be more challenging, but progress can still be made with patience and consistent effort.

Model healthy emotional regulation. Children learn by observing their parents, so it's essential to demonstrate how to constructively manage emotions. When you experience emotions, share them with your child and show them how you cope. A responsive, warm, and accepting parenting style helps emotional development. When your child is distressed, responding to their emotional needs and comforting them helps create a secure attachment. Validate their feelings, offer support, and encourage open communication.

The overall emotional climate in the family significantly impacts a child's self-regulating ability. A positive and consistent emotional environment promotes emotional security. Conversely, an adverse climate marked by frequent displays of negative emotions like anger or hostility can hinder a child's development.

As your kids grow older, start teaching them self-regulation techniques. These techniques can be applied at different stages of emotion generation, including redirecting attention, reframing situations, and practicing coping skills. Self-care activities such as exercise, mindfulness, adequate sleep, and relaxation techniques can enhance a child's internal resources for emotional regulation. Encourage your child to engage in these activities as part of their daily routine.

Why Kids Learn from Parents' Emotions

You are your kid's first and most influential teacher, shaping their understanding of the world in countless ways. One of the most essential aspects of this teaching role is how your emotions impact your children's learning and development.

Emotions are remarkably contagious, and your children are like sponges, soaking up the feelings you express. When your child observes you experiencing specific emotions, they are highly likely to mirror them. For example, if you become angry, your child is more likely to feel anger. This emotional mirroring is an essential part of their learning process.

Why does this happen? Well, it's because emotions provide valuable information about the world. Your child learns what's important, what's acceptable, and how to react to various situations by watching your emotional responses. They learn that honesty is valued if you become upset when they lie. This connection between your emotions and their understanding of right and wrong is crucial in their moral development.

Moreover, emotions are a bridge for forming connections. When your child sees you express your feelings, it reassures them that emotions are okay. They learn that they're not alone, and this understanding helps them develop strong emotional bonds with you and others.

You might wonder how this emotional learning connects to your child's development. Well, it's a key ingredient in various aspects of their growth. For instance, it helps them learn how to identify and label their emotions, which helps them to have healthy emotional development. When they see you show joy, sadness, anger, or fear, they learn the words to describe these emotions, which expands their vocabulary.

Furthermore, children learn to express their emotions healthily by observing your reactions. If you constructively handle your emotions, like calming down before responding, consciously or unconsciously, they will learn to do likewise. That way, you help set an example for them to effectively manage their emotions. When your child sees you empathizing with others, they begin to see the importance of considering others' feelings. This will help them build strong, positive relationships as they grow.

Stress is a part of life, and children encounter it, too. However, they might not always know how to handle it. How you handle stress and stressors can also help them to deal with stress and difficult emotions. If they see you managing stress positively, it sets an example for them to follow.

Moreover, your emotional expressions help your child build a sense of self. As they see you express joy when they accomplish something or disappointment when they make a mistake, they better understand their strengths and weaknesses. This self-awareness is an essential foundation for personal growth.

Your emotions also offer insight into what's important in your family and culture. For example, if you celebrate certain events joyfully, your child learns the significance of those occasions. This cultural and familial context shapes their values and beliefs.

As your child grows, they enter a social world where emotions play a crucial role in interactions. By learning from your emotional responses, they gain valuable insights into how to navigate this social landscape. They discover the nuances of social interactions and learn what's considered appropriate behavior in different contexts.

Furthermore, your emotional expressions impact your child's self-image. When they see you express pride in their achievements or offer comfort when they're feeling down, it boosts their self-esteem. These positive emotional interactions help them develop a positive self-image, which is important for their well-being.

In addition to all these, life will inevitably present challenges, and understanding and managing their emotions will help them bounce back from adversity and become better equipped to face life's ups and downs.

Emotional learning from parents contributes to happier and healthier adults. When you provide your child with a solid emotional foundation, you strengthen them to face life's challenges, build meaningful relationships, and develop into well-rounded individuals.

It's important to acknowledge that no one is perfect, including parents. You'll undoubtedly experience and express negative emotions at times. However, the key is how you manage these emotions. For example, imagine a situation where you feel anger. Instead of reacting impulsively, take a moment to calm down and gather your thoughts. Show your child that it's okay to feel anger, but it's also important to manage it constructively. You can explain to them why you felt angry and how you're handling it, emphasizing the importance of finding healthy outlets for negative emotions.

Conversations about emotions are important. Encourage your child to talk about their feelings and concerns. When they see you constructively discussing your emotions, it sets a positive example for open communication. This, in turn, helps them feel safe and supported in expressing their emotions.

Practicing Emotion Regulation Together

When children come across new emotions, they usually don't know what these feelings mean or the context in which they arise. This is where verbal feedback and intonation come into play. When you give simple, descriptive feedback, you help your child associate their emotions with specific experiences. For instance, saying, "Wow, you were jumping with excitement," or "You're looking sad," connects the emotion to a recognizable context.

As your child continues to experience these emotions, they begin to form associations between the emotion, its meaning, and the context in which it occurs. This process is basic to their emotional development.

Many children learn about emotions by becoming aware of the physical sensations accompanying different feelings. These bodily sensations can vary from person to person. For instance, when your child experiences anxiety or worry, they might describe it as a tingling sensation in the stomach or tight fists and clenched toes.

If your child tends to have intense emotional reactions, it would be very helpful to help them recognize the early bodily sensations associated with these emotions. By naming these sensations, you empower your child to become more aware of their emotional responses. For instance, if they know that a tingling in the stomach signifies anxiety, they'll be better equipped to identify and address it. However, it's important to note that some children might need repeated practice to develop this.

Successful self-regulation serves several key purposes: It helps your child manage intense emotions and find balance when they experience strong feelings. Children who can regulate their emotions are more likely to feel good about themselves, reducing feelings of shame and anxiety related to emotional struggles.

Emotional self-regulation is key to building and maintaining positive friendships and relationships. It helps children to go through social interactions more effectively. It also contributes to your child's success in school by helping them build concentration, effective communication, and the ability to handle challenges with a calm and focused mindset.

Below, we've highlighted some practical activities and strategies to help your child develop and practice emotional self-regulation. Mood cards can be very helpful in teaching your kids how to express their emotions and how others perceive them. You can create mood cards by printing and cutting out pictures of people displaying specific emotions.

Place these pictures in a bag and have your child pick one at a time. Encourage them to name, describe, and perhaps even identify with the emotion depicted in the picture. Then, ask them to share a personal experience related to that emotion. What did they do when they felt this way? Did things go as expected? Are there better ways they could have handled the emotion? This activity helps your child identify and label their emotions and encourages them to reflect on their emotional responses and consider alternative ways to manage their feelings in the future.

One overlooked but helpful strategy is picture books. Reading picture books or discussing stories is one excellent way to enhance your child's emotional intelligence. Choose books with vivid illustrations and ask your child to describe the emotions conveyed by the characters. Encourage them to speculate about why the characters feel that way and how they might react in similar situations. This practice builds their emotional vocabulary and helps them understand the complexities of human emotions.

Board games are also excellent for practicing emotional regulation skills. Choose games that are enjoyable but not overly complex to start with. Games like Uno, which involve turn-taking and impulse control, are great choices. When your kids play these games, they naturally develop patience, flexibility in thinking, and the ability to cope with winning and losing. This helps them regulate emotions effectively in real-life situations.

The Incredible 5-Point Scale, designed by Kari Dunn Buron, is a structured approach to emotion regulation that can be personalized to your child's emotions and situations. The scale ranges from 1 to 5, with 1 indicating a mild intensity of emotion and 5 representing an intense emotional state. Work with your child to identify what different emotions look and feel like at each level of intensity. Once the scale is established, you can help your child take action to move from one level to another.

For example, suppose your child is about to perform on stage at a school concert and feels excitement at level 4. They might use deep, slow breathing or repetitive, rhythmic movements to bring their excitement down to level 2 or 1. This structured approach empowers your child to manage their emotions proactively and preventatively.

The Zones of Regulation is a visual approach to understanding and categorizing emotions. It uses colors to represent emotional states:

- The Red Zone signifies extremely heightened emotions like anger, rage, or panic.

- The Yellow Zone represents heightened alertness and elevated emotions, which a child has more control over.
- The Green Zone indicates a calm and focused state, ideal for learning and following instructions.
- The Blue Zone represents low alertness and feelings like sadness, tiredness, and boredom.

Encourage your child to identify their zone and express their desire to shift to another zone. This visual framework helps them recognize and control their emotional states more effectively.

Emotional regulation is a long road that travels to adulthood, and you just have to be patient and realistic in your expectations. To make it easier, you can increase your awareness of your emotional responses and label them when talking to your child. When you help them model healthy emotional expression, they are better able to understand various emotions.

Ensure your child has a designated safe space where they can go to feel calm and comforted when their emotions run high. This safe haven can also help their emotional regulation. Create regular opportunities to chat with your child without pressure. Car rides, cooking, or walking together can be good moments to discuss emotions and experiences.

Be present and offer your undivided attention when your child struggles with intense emotions. Make eye contact, listen without distraction, and show them you are there for them and with them. Your presence can help ground them and make them feel safe. You must also recognize that your child's ability to manage emotions can vary depending on factors like tiredness, blood sugar levels, and environment. Avoid expecting perfection and understand that sometimes they struggle to regulate their emotions.

Healthy sleep patterns, a balanced diet, and regular exercise are a big part of successful self-regulation. Focus on making small, manageable changes to support your child's emotional well-being.

Empathy and Validation in Parenting

Empathy and validation in parenting are not just buzzwords; they can profoundly impact your child's emotional development and strengthen your parent-child bond. Empathy is not simply agreeing with your child's feelings; it's about understanding and sharing emotions. You approach the situation from their shoes, acknowledge their real and valid feelings, and offer support. Validation, in this context, means recognizing and affirming that your child's emotions and experiences are worthwhile, even if you don't necessarily agree with their actions.

Imagine your child coming to you with a problem or strong emotion. Before I learned about validation, I instinctively provided a quick solution. However, I soon realized that my children weren't always seeking answers; many times, they just wanted to be heard and understood. Invalidation, on the other hand, can be unintentional but detrimental. It's when we dismiss, judge, or ignore our child's emotional experiences. This can happen when we rush to reassure them, saying things like, "Don't be sad," or "It'll be okay," thinking we're helping when, in fact, we're invalidating their feelings.

For instance, when my daughter felt upset about her body image at age six, responding with "That's ridiculous," would have invalidated her feelings. Instead, we had a daddy-daughter talk, which helped her express her emotions and why she felt that way. Children often feel invalidated when adults dictate their emotional responses. Phrases like "Don't be angry, honey," or "You can't be hungry; we just ate," might seem harmless but can invalidate a child's perception and emotions. This habit stems from our lack of exposure to empathy and validation in our upbringing.

Invalidation can lead children to doubt their instincts and rely on external approval, weakening their "inner compass" and, invariably, their self-esteem. Unacknowledged emotions might resurface in covert or repressed ways later in life. When you validate your child's emotions, you build trust and show them that their thoughts and feelings matter. You teach them that their mind and body signals are valuable. Validation and empathy usually work better than suppression or fixing the problem because they help children move away from heightened emotional states.

When you validate your child, it begins to calm them. Without validation, they might not realize you heard them and remain in fight-or-flight mode. Once they feel understood, they can transition to a calmer mental state. This process communicates that you take them seriously and can handle their emotions without imposing your needs.

Validation also creates cooperation and teamwork. Instead of engaging in power struggles, you can work together to discuss issues and reach a consensus, creating a stronger relationship.

Validating your child's emotions might not always come naturally, especially if you haven't experienced it much, but you can reflect their feelings. Use phrases like, "It sounds like you were frustrated when..."

or "I'm guessing you're feeling disappointed right now." Reflecting on their emotions helps them feel understood.

Let your child know that their emotions are normal. For instance, say, "It's okay to feel nervous about starting a new school." Avoid immediately jumping to reassurance. During intense emotional moments, ignore the behavior and focus on the emotion. Once your child calms down, praise their coping or perseverance.

You can also show your child how you deal with emotions. Say, "I'm feeling very frustrated. It's okay to feel this way. I'll take a break and return to this when I'm calmer." This models acceptance of emotions and healthy coping. Find spaces where your feelings are heard and validated to better validate your child. Share with your partner, talk to other parents, or seek supportive communities.

Validation is often overlooked in traditional parenting approaches, which focus more on behavior management. Children who struggle with emotion regulation are at a higher risk of developing mental health issues like anxiety and depression. By validating your child's emotional experiences, you help them handle intense emotions effectively. This, in turn, reduces tantrums, meltdowns, and conflicts within the family. Teaching children to self-regulate is a vital parenting task because emotion regulation is a life skill that predicts positive outcomes.

Validation doesn't mean you endorse their actions; it means you accept their feelings. It de-escalates emotionally charged situations, allowing your child to feel heard and understood. When children are validated, the intensity of their emotions decreases, enabling them to move through difficult moments more swiftly and make better decisions.

Moreover, validation enhances emotional intelligence. Children who can effectively label their emotions are more likely to communicate their experiences calmly rather than resort to aggressive behavior or tantrums. This leads to more supportive and accepting relationships and promotes healthy self-esteem.

Validating your child's emotions can be tough, especially when their distress triggers your own. You need to stay calm, especially if your child is aggressive or destructive. Validation is about allowing your child to sit with their emotions and acknowledge them. It's not about fixing problems or changing their emotional experience. Validation shows that you are there, trying to understand and willing to support them.

Sometimes, validation is as simple as being present. It demonstrates that their emotions are not too big for you to handle and that you are ready to help when they are calm.

Incorporating empathy and validation into your parenting approach can transform your relationship with your child and help their emotional well-being. When you understand the power of empathy, acknowledge the importance of validation, and implement practical steps for validation, you can guide your child through the challenges of growing up with compassion and support.

Validation isn't just about your child, it's also about modeling positive coping skills and fostering emotional intelligence. As you validate your child's emotions, you help them to trust their instincts and develop the critical life skill of emotion regulation. A culture of empathy and validation in your home creates a foundation for a resilient, emotionally intelligent, and well-adjusted child. Your efforts today will have a lasting positive impact on your child's future.

Teaching Children to Express Their Emotions

Beyond understanding your kids' emotions, you must also teach them how to express them. The relationship between behavior and the capacity to express emotion is complex and significant. Kids often act out when they find it hard to verbally communicate their feelings. This is particularly pronounced in younger children, especially those under the age of five.

For children below the age of two, their limited language skills might lead to possessive behaviors, especially toward people and objects they hold dear. These young children could become easily frustrated, leading to shouting or throwing things to convey their emotions.

At the age of three, children might have developed a broader vocabulary. However, they still experience sudden mood swings and engage in extreme behaviors without fully understanding why they feel this way.

By age five, most children can typically express and manage their feelings to some extent. However, some continue to grapple with this skill, and this difficulty could be linked to underlying factors such as Special Educational Needs and Disabilities (SEND). Conditions like Autism Spectrum Disorder, speech and language difficulties, or social, emotional, and mental health needs such as anxiety can hinder their ability to articulate their emotions. Instead of verbal expression, these children might frequently cry or experience tantrums, aggression, persistent worrying, frustration, difficulty letting go, or sudden bursts of energy.

Teaching children about emotions and encouraging them to express their feelings is transformative. It equips them with the vocabulary and tools to communicate their inner world, fostering emotional intelligence and healthier behavior. Children with high emotional intelligence tend to be more empathic and supportive. Emotional intelligence is also linked to improved mental health and reduced risk of anxiety. When children can express their emotions effectively, they are more likely to exhibit appropriate behavior. Emotional intelligence strengthens interpersonal relationships in childhood and adulthood.

Children with emotional intelligence often perform better in school and have improved career prospects. Allowing children to express themselves communicates that you value their feelings, showing that you will listen and not undermine their emotions.

Help your child associate feelings with words by consistently labeling emotions until they can do it independently. Use books, photos, and videos to discuss facial expressions and emotions experienced by others. Consider choosing literature that sparks emotional discussions during reading time, like the picture books I mentioned earlier.

Drawing, painting, and coloring can allow children to express their emotions visually. Some children might find it easier to draw what they think their emotions look like, aiding their emotional processing and allowing you to better understand their feelings.

You should also learn to recognize and respond promptly to your child's emotional cues. This two-way process involves reading their signals and providing a supportive response. Avoid invalidating or dismissing their feelings (I'm saying that again).

Encourage children to express their feelings through non-verbal means when verbal expression is challenging. Dance, running, singing, or deep breathing can help release emotional energy. Use tools like feelings boards and scales to facilitate discussions about emotions.

Please remain approachable to your children. Maintain open body language, friendly facial expressions, and kind words to make them feel secure. Show that you can listen and engage actively in conversations about their feelings. Young children might not fully grasp the impact of their actions on others, so help them recognize this by pointing out how their behavior can affect others. When conflicts arise, listen to both perspectives and discuss the needs and feelings of each party involved.

Role-Playing to Improve Parent-Child Interactions

You've likely witnessed your child's fascination with role-play (I've had to be Prince Charming for my girl a number of times). The way they create dialogues and transform everyday objects into props to suit their imagination is fascinating. But do you know how role play affects their personality and logical development?

When adults encounter a problem or need to consider another person's perspective, more often than not, we reason things out in our heads. But where do children develop these tools for objective thought? The foundation for logical skills like perspective-taking begins with activities like role-play. For children, acting out various roles is like asking themselves how someone else might think and react in a given situation.

Although children perceive it as play, it's a great way to help them understand and empathize with different viewpoints. In many ways, role-playing builds logical, diplomatic, and empathic abilities.

Among the many role-playing games children enjoy, playing house is a favorite. It's pretty simple: Kids try to be what they have observed in the family. Through playing house, children play the roles of mothers and fathers, influenced by their families, books, and media depictions. Playing house with friends from different family backgrounds also expands their notion of family, encouraging inclusivity and understanding.

Children also get involved in role-playing to show you what profession they think will suit them when they grow up. They can wear a firefighter's hat or a doctor's coat or do pretend rescues or diagnoses. While career aspirations might change, this early exploration is much needed for their development.

Role-playing is an integral component of early childhood development because it aids children in comprehending the world and their peers. Next time you observe your child donning a whimsical costume and adopting a character's persona, remember they're honing logical and emotional skills. You can even join in the fun.

Have you ever noticed your child pretending to answer your phone or commandeering a TV remote control as if it were a car? Have you ever wondered what goes on in their curious minds? The advantages of role-playing for children extend far beyond mere entertainment. Child therapists often use role-play therapy to help children deal with tough situations and even address autism.

Role-playing fuels creativity and enhances problem-solving abilities and performance in school. It helps children to take up characters that simulate real-life roles, teaching them essential life skills.

Role-playing is closely linked to cognitive flexibility and creativity. It nurtures a child's capacity for cognitive flexibility, allowing them to exercise their imagination early on. This creativity is pivotal in problem-solving and shapes their ability to appreciate literature, plan for life's pleasures, and empathize with diverse perspectives. Albert Einstein aptly stated, "Logic will get you from A to Z, but imagination will get you everywhere."

Children are rapid learners, swiftly assimilating new words and concepts, especially when connected to characters they like. Role-play allows them to experiment with new vocabulary, expanding their linguistic abilities. Through this language immersion, they build confidence in communication, learn to convey their thoughts, and, in turn, become adept listeners. These skills can help them get better in reading and writing proficiency.

During the role-play, children enter imaginative social scenarios that require them to interact and collaborate. This experience allows children to relate to others' emotions and gain control over their reactions; that's emotional regulation. Furthermore, role-playing equips them with vital conflict-resolution skills as they work together to find solutions.

Beyond its cognitive and emotional benefits, role-playing also significantly impacts a child's physical development. When you observe your child dashing around to "save the day" or climbing ladders to extinguish imaginary fires, they are engaging their motor skills and enhancing hand-eye coordination. This active play contributes to their physical well-being and overall development.

To get them going on role-play, dedicate a secure indoor or outdoor area filled with stuffed animals, costumes, and props to foster imagination. You can even join them by becoming a character. This involvement strengthens your bond and enriches your experience.

Reading stories playfully and interactively, using a child's tone, and posing open-ended questions stimulate their creativity. Bedtime stories in particular offer an excellent opportunity for imaginative exploration. Allow your child to lead in role-playing scenarios that will help them determine the narrative and freely exercise their creativity.

Practical Worksheet: Our Emotion Regulation Action Plan

Guidelines for Using Emotional Regulation Action Plans

These guidelines will help you and your child effectively use the Emotional Regulation Action Plan:

- This plan belongs to your child and should be developed when calm.
- It should be done between your child and a person or people with whom there is a relationship or a sense of trust.
- The plan should be reviewed monthly between your child and the adult guide.
- As an ongoing well-being plan, things identified as triggers or supports can be added, and things can be removed if found to be not accurate or unsuccessful.
- The plan should grow with your child.

Identifying Behavior Concerns (Circle all that apply)

- Losing my temper
- Fighting/hurting people
- Withdrawing
- Running away

- Injuring myself
- Threatening others
- Swearing
- Damaging property
- Throwing things
- Leaving the classroom
- Other: _____

Identifying Triggers

- Not being listened to
- Feeling pressured
- Being touched
- People yelling
- Feeling lonely
- Feeling left out
- Being stared at
- Teasing
- Not having a say
- Particular class/subject
- Contact with: _____
- Not understanding work
- Arguments
- The particular time of day
- Other: _____

Recognizing Warning Signs

- Sweating
- Red face
- Acting hyper
- Being rude
- Singing/humming
- Breathing heavy
- Wringing hands
- Swearing
- Pacing
- Becoming very quiet
- Loud voice
- Bouncing legs
- Crying
- Hygiene issues
- Clenching teeth
- Rocking
- Squatting
- Damaging things
- Hurting myself
- Isolating/avoiding others
- Other: _____

Possible Ways to Regulate My Feelings
- **What Works:**
  - Time to myself
  - Listening to music
  - Singing softly
  - Sitting with staff
  - Pacing in private
  - Talking with a support person
  - Coloring, playing with clay
  - Reading a book
  - Run, fast walk, jumping jacks
  - A cold splash of water
  - Writing in a journal
  - Punching a pillow
  - Humor
  - Push-ups, sit-ups
  - Bouncing a ball
  - Drawing
  - Being around other people
  - Hugging a stuffed animal
  - Playing cards
  - Talking to staff:
  - Holding an ice cube

- Deep breathing
- Calling: _____
- Using the sensory room
- Lying down
- Snapping a rubber band
- Using the gym
- Being in nature
- My designated safe space: _____
- Telling myself to relax
- Hearing hopeful messages
- Rocking or swinging

What to Try:

_____

_____

Things That Make It Worse for Me

- Being alone
- Being around people
- Humor
- Not being listened to
- Peers teasing
- Being disrespected
- Loud tone of voice

- Being ignored
- Having staff support
- Talking to an adult
- Being touched
- Being reminded of the rules
- Other: _____

Creating an Emotional Regulation Plan

- **When I Notice These Warning Signs and Triggers:**

  _____

  _____

- **I Will:**

  _____

  _____

  - to prevent a crisis from developing.

- **When Staff Notices:**

  _____

  _____

- **I Would Like Them to Help Prevent a Crisis by:**

  _____

  _____

- **When I Follow This Plan, I Will Reward Myself by:**

  _____

- Other Ideas About What to Do if a Crisis Develops:

  _____

  _____

People on My Support Team

Include names, phone numbers, and emails of individuals on your child's support team such as school staff, therapists, family, and friends.

Name	Phone	Email

Takeaway Five

- Children's emotional experiences evolve as they age, and different age groups require varying forms of support. Infants rely heavily on pre-wired emotional responses during the first months of life. They cry to signal discomfort or seek pleasurable stimuli like food and physical contact.

- Emotional regulation is not a skill we are born with, it is a learned ability that profoundly impacts a child's life. Poor emotional regulation can lead to frequent tantrums, strained parent-child relationships, and difficulty forming and maintaining friendships. In contrast, strong emotional regulation skills contribute to improved relationships, academic success, and overall well-being.

- Children learn by observing their parents, so it is essential to demonstrate how to constructively manage emotions. When you experience emotions, share them with your child and show them how you cope.
- Stress is a part of life, and children encounter it, too. However, they might not always know how to handle it. Modeling how you handle stress and stressors can help them to deal with stress and difficult emotions. If they see you managing stress positively, it sets an example for them to follow.
- Successful self-regulation serves several key purposes including helping your child to manage intense emotions and finding balance when they experience strong feelings. Children who can regulate their emotions are more likely to feel good about themselves, reducing feelings of shame and anxiety related to emotional struggles.

PART THREE
Building a Happy and Resilient Family

~~~

A happy family might sound like a fairy tale. It probably gets you thinking of Elsa and Anna, the two princess sisters from Frozen. Always there for each other, no matter what, supporting each other through thick and thin. The beautiful thing is that this kind of family does not just exist in movies; it is real, and you can have it, too. A happy and resilient family can weather the storms of life and come out even stronger on the other side. It is a family where everyone feels loved, supported, and respected, communication is open and honest, and problems are solved together.

Perfectionism can be a major obstacle to building a happy and resilient family. When perfection is the main focus, you might begin to place unrealistic expectations on yourself and your children, and it will lead to stress, anxiety, and conflict. Nothing can replace the parent-child bond. Not only is it fulfilling, but it helps your child grow up balanced and well-rounded, especially emotionally. When you have a close relationship with your children, you are more likely to support each other through difficult times. In this part, you will learn how to communicate effectively, spend quality time together, and show love and affection.

There will be ups and downs along the way. But when you embrace imperfection, strengthen your relationships, and focus on gratitude, you can thrive despite imperfections. In the last chapter, I will explain the importance of finding peace and happiness. You will also learn how to let go of negative emotions, focus on the positive, and become better.

I'm so happy you've made it this far. I can't wait to see you at the end.

CHAPTER SIX

Overcoming Perfectionism

"Better to do something imperfectly than to do nothing flawlessly."

— Robert Schuller

"My grace is sufficient for you, for My strength is made perfect in weakness."

— 2 Corinthians 12:9 (NKJV)

I grew up with a dad who was passionate about Go. He taught my sister and me how to play when we were kids and even started a Go club at our school. One day, for reasons I'll never understand, he enrolled me in Go lessons with the state champion. Every week, I would go to these lessons and study all the moves to win against an opponent with different combinations of pieces.

I couldn't analyze the board the way my dad did, though. He could look at the board and tell me exactly what I should have done five moves back to *be in a winning position. He could even memorize the way the board looked throughout the game.*

I could memorize the prescribed moves and theories for the endgame, and I learned to trade pieces instead of pawns in the middle game, but I knew I would never be as good as my dad.

Eventually, I gave up on Go.

~Anabelle

The Perfectionist Parenting Dilemma

Case Study

Lisa was the perfect wife and mother. Every task was meticulously planned and perfectly executed. Her home was spotless, and her boss mentioned yesterday that she was an asset to the company. Her child's school's PTA board was happy that she was the chair. They had achieved a lot, thanks to her. The goal was to be perfect, and she was meeting it, or so people thought. Beneath Lisa's flawless exterior, self-doubt and anxiety brewed.

Praise from friends and colleagues felt hollow, overshadowed by the fear of failure that loomed over her. No matter how much she achieved, it was never enough to silence the critical voice in her head.

Although she kept pushing herself to keep up with appearances, deep down, she wanted freedom from the impossible standards she'd set for herself.

But what Lisa worried about the most as she kissed her daughter's forehead goodnight was that she was passing her perfectionistic tendencies to her daughter. And she somehow felt that her daughter would live this kind of life, working herself to the bone to be perfect.

We live in a world where it often feels like everyone is watching and judging our every move. From social media trolls criticizing your choices to well-meaning friends offering unsolicited advice, the pressure to be perfect parents is always there. We want the best for our children, and that desire can sometimes lead into perfectionism. But here's the truth: Striving for perfection stresses you out and can harm your child's well-being.

Perfectionist parents come in different forms. Some are perfectionists in all aspects of life, excelling at everything they do but never feeling quite good enough. Others reserve their perfectionism solely for parenting, fearing they'll "mess up" their children's lives if they fall short.

If you are a perfectionist parent, you tend to hold yourself to incredibly high standards. You believe that you must do well in every aspect of parenting from discipline to taking care of the bills, and even cleaning and cooking. As a result, you criticize yourself for any perceived shortcomings. This self-criticism can manifest as feelings of inadequacy and anxiety. It can also lead to a constant sense of dissatisfaction, as it is almost impossible to meet your standards.

When a perfectionist parent's child has an issue (let's say a health challenge) or doesn't do well enough (at school, for example), the parent might be quick to blame themselves. They could feel that their inability to create a perfect environment or make flawless decisions is the cause of their child's problems.

Perfectionist parents often compare themselves to other parents. This habit can be damaging because it doesn't consider the unique circumstances and needs of the family. You just want to be validated by others and measure your success based on what you see other families do. Comparing yourself to others can fuel insecurity and undermine your confidence.

Another sign that you might be a perfectionist is that you overextend yourself more often than not. You feel you should be able to handle everything, often taking on more responsibilities than you can reasonably manage. Of course, you can become burned out, stressed, and exhausted, and this in turn can negatively impact your ability to parent effectively. There is also second-guessing when you constantly question whether you are making the right decisions for your children. This breeds a high level of stress and uncertainty, as your kids might find it difficult to trust your instincts, decisions, and judgment.

The pressure of being a perfectionist parent can sometimes result in frustration and losing one's temper. When things don't go as planned or when your children don't meet the high expectations you've set, you can get outbursts of anger or impatience. The kids are also not left out, since most perfectionists extend the traits and standards to those around them. You might find it difficult to watch your child do something if it's not done your way. You could also tend to micromanage your child's tasks and activities, leaving them little room for independence.

If you are a perfectionist, your child might feel pressured to perform flawlessly in academics, sports, or other activities because you find it easier to criticize your child than to praise them, focusing on their mistakes. Consciously or unconsciously, you push your child to fulfill your unfulfilled dreams or aspirations. This is because your self-worth is closely tied to your child's achievements, adding immense pressure to the already overburdened child.

Perfectionist parenting affects many, but it appears to impact working mothers disproportionately. There are a couple of reasons behind this. First, if you are accustomed to high achievement in your career, you could feel the need to excel in all other aspects of life, including parenting.

Second, working mothers often experience heightened stress as they juggle multiple roles. Dads are not immune to parenting guilt. A Pew Research Center survey from 2015 revealed that nearly half of all fathers did not give themselves high marks as parents. Even though today's fathers spend significantly more time with their children than those in the past, they still feel they aren't doing enough.

Now, we need to differentiate between having high standards and being a perfectionist. While high standards can motivate children to succeed, perfectionist parenting sets unrealistic expectations that can harm a child's well-being. Perfectionist parenting makes children believe that they're failures if they don't achieve the highest standards. This pressure can lead to cheating and dishonesty, as they might believe achievement is more valued than honesty.

Kids raised with perfectionist expectations are at a higher risk of developing mental health issues including depression, anxiety, and eating disorders. These problems often go untreated because children might hide their symptoms.

Paradoxically, expecting perfection tends to decrease a child's performance. When the bar is set impossibly high, children might give up rather than strive for unattainable goals. Perfectionism is also linked to self-defeating behavior such as procrastination. Ironically, it increases the likelihood of failure rather than success.

DBT Techniques for Letting Go of Perfection

Fortunately, Dialectical Behavior Therapy (DBT) can help you let go of perfectionism and lead a more fulfilling life. These techniques are not a quick fix but a deliberate effort toward self-discovery and growth. When you let go of your relentless pursuit of perfection, you can rest, relax, and enjoy parenthood.

The first step in letting go of perfectionism is self-awareness. You can't solve a problem if you are not aware it exists. Take a moment to reflect on your thoughts and emotions when you're faced with tasks or goals related to parenting. Do you often find yourself criticizing your actions, thinking you're never good enough? Are your expectations for yourself and your child impossibly high? Take a moment to reflect on your day-to-day parenting experiences. Notice the moments when you're overly critical of yourself or when you set unrealistic standards for your child or yourself. Can you identify patterns? Awareness is the first step toward change, and when you can spot perfectionistic tendencies as they arise, it becomes much easier to tackle them.

Once you've identified your perfectionistic thoughts, it's time to question their validity. Ask yourself if these thoughts are realistic or helpful. Do you demand perfection even when it's unattainable? Are your standards too high? You can contest these thoughts by reminding yourself that everyone — including you — makes mistakes, and it's okay to be imperfect.

Self-compassion is one skill I advise you to cultivate. We are often quicker to extend a hand of grace to others than we are to ourselves. Imagine how you would comfort and support a friend who's going through a tough time. Now, extend that same kindness and understanding to yourself. When you're feeling judgmental or disappointed with your parenting, remember that you're human, and humans make mistakes.

Rather than striving for unattainable perfection, shift your focus toward making progress. Celebrate the small victories along the way and don't be too hard on yourself when you face setbacks. Parenthood is a journey of growth, and it's perfectly normal to learn and evolve at your own pace. Your child is also on a unique path of development, and together, you can learn and grow.

Perfectionism comes from the notion that you must be perfect to be worthy of love and respect. Most perfectionists believe that being anything less than perfect would take them off the radar of love and acceptance. However, that is not at all true: Imperfection is an inherent part of the human experience. When you can accept your imperfections, you'll find that stress and anxiety begin to loosen their grip on your life.

Mindfulness is a core component of DBT that can be incredibly helpful in letting go of perfectionism. Mindfulness is simply enjoying the moment, reliving every moment, and actively staying in the present. As a parent, practicing mindfulness can help you become more aware of your perfectionistic tendencies as they arise. It allows you to observe your thoughts and emotions without getting caught up in them, which can also aid your self-awareness. When you notice perfectionism creeping in, gently guide your focus back to the present moment.

Sometimes, you need to give yourself a break from the pressure of perfectionism. Yep, perfectionism can mount intense and unnecessary pressure on you. DBT helps you distract yourself from these thoughts and practice self-soothing activities. Find something enjoyable that helps you relax and take your mind off the need to be perfect. It can be something simple such as reading a book, taking a walk, or watching your favorite show. These activities can provide a much-needed respite from the constant drive for perfection.

Another valuable DBT technique is setting realistic goals. Rather than aiming for perfection in every aspect of your life, break your goals into smaller, more achievable steps. This approach not only reduces the pressure you put on yourself but also makes it easier to track your progress.

Radical acceptance is fully acknowledging and accepting reality, even when it's not what you'd prefer. In this approach, you let go of the need to control every outcome and recognize that some things are beyond your control. As a parent, there will be moments of unpredictability and imperfection: Choose to see them as part of the beautiful mess of parenthood.

Building Self-Confidence as a Parent

Parenthood is filled with highs and lows, laughter and tears. You'll get your fair share of self-assuredness and self-doubt. There are days when your emotions get the better of you, and you might react in ways you later regret. You might raise your voice, give in to unreasonable demands, or find yourself overwhelmed and on the brink of tears.

We all have those days, but what matters to your child is that you do a good enough job. Let's be clear: This doesn't mean you condone abusive or neglectful behavior. Instead, it means that you are okay with the fact that you will have days when you feel like you're doing a lousy job, and that's okay. Parenting is not about being perfect, it's about being present and willing to learn and grow over time.

One significant factor that can affect your confidence as a parent is self-esteem. If you struggle with low self-esteem, it can affect your ability to parent effectively. Low self-esteem makes you hesitant in decision-making and brings constant self-doubt about whether you're making the right choices for your child.

Low self-esteem can also come from hurtful experiences like childhood abuse or neglect, overly critical parents, feelings of rejection, or overprotective caregivers. These experiences can give you an incorrect view of yourself and can lead to negative feelings such as feeling unworthy, unlovable, or powerless.

These negative feelings and beliefs are internal "I" statements that we unconsciously make. Some common negative core beliefs include:

- I am unworthy.
- I am unlovable.
- I am unwanted.
- I don't belong.
- I am powerless.
- I am nothing.
- I am not real.
- I am defective.
- I am worthless.
- I am unsafe.
- I am not whole.

If these sound like you, then you need to reflect on when you first noticed these statements and what was happening in your life at that time. This can help identify the root cause of these beliefs. Once you recognize the origin, it will be much easier to remove it.

You might ask what exactly your children need from you. Children need parents who can be bigger, stronger, wiser, and kinder. Bigger means providing warmth, affection, and kindness while maintaining a strong sense of being in charge. It's about being firm yet compassionate, setting boundaries, and explaining rules in an empathetic way.

Children need parents who can be their emotional support when they face challenges. That is what makes your parenting stronger. They look up to you as a source of strength and guidance. Your ability to positively handle your emotions will teach them how to manage theirs.

As a parent, you bring wisdom and life experience to the table. Use it to guide your child, teach them life lessons, and help them understand the world. Kindness is a cornerstone of effective parenting. Show empathy and understanding toward your child's emotions, even when they're difficult.

Now that we've laid the groundwork let's learn some practical steps to boost your self-confidence as a parent. Regularly examine your thoughts, feelings, and actions as a parent. Focus on what you did well and what you can improve upon. Reflecting on your parenting experiences helps you grow. While it's advisable to seek guidance and support from trusted sources, remember that not all advice applies to your situation. Learn to filter comments and suggestions, accepting only what complements your parenting style.

A secure attachment between you and your child begins with creating a safe space for them to share their feelings. Practice "being with" your child during their emotional moments, showing empathy and understanding. Strive to be a parent who combines kindness with clear boundaries and rules. Being firm but kind can foster independence and self-esteem in your child.

Taking care of yourself physically and mentally can boost your self-confidence. Proper nutrition, exercise, and rest can help you stay balanced and better equipped to handle the challenges of parenting. Keep yourself informed about the latest parenting insights and research. Reading books and articles, and joining parenting communities can provide valuable knowledge and support.

Confidence begins with believing in yourself. Trust your instincts, learn from your mistakes, and remind yourself that you are capable of being the parent your child needs. You've got this, and remember, there's no such thing as a perfect parent, but there are countless opportunities to be a loving, nurturing, and confident one.

Setting Realistic Expectations for Yourself and Your Child

My son recently took a math test at school, and he scored 15 out of 20. He handed me his test score and then asked me this question with a tinge of innocence: "Is this considered good?" I was taken aback and a host of questions ran through my mind. Had I been too hard on him? How did he get the notion that I placed that much expectation on him? I carefully considered my response to him and finally said, "I think you tried your best, so I guess it's not bad." His question turned into a reflection of myself, even if I'm not sure whether I answered it well.

Now, I want to ask you, what are your expectations for your child? What do you consider a "good" result? If your child scored 15 out of 20, would you praise or criticize? Most of us want the best for our children. Notice that I used the word "want." Our desires and wishes for our children's future attainment often take precedence over what we realistically expect them to achieve.

Sometimes, our strong desires for academic excellence can inadvertently lead to unrealistic expectations. Some parents relentlessly push their children to achieve top grades, while others react strongly when their children make mistakes and fall short of expectations. I've met children who, despite scoring 98 out of 100, were still upset because they made careless errors. Some were worried about facing their parents' disappointment. Heartbreakingly, I've heard children say that nothing they do is ever good enough for their parents.

If this mentality continues, it can have detrimental effects on children's self-esteem. They might become overly concerned about making mistakes or failing to meet high standards imposed by others, including parents and teachers. This fear of making errors and falling short of expectations is known as maladaptive perfectionism. Research shows that individuals high in maladaptive perfectionism often experience anxiety, depression, and burnout over the long term. I'm sure this is the last thing any parent would want for their child.

Your child is an individual, so to set realistic expectations, you must consider their strengths, weaknesses, interests, and talents. Avoid relying solely on charts, statistics, and data to gauge your child's progress because every child develops at their own pace. Each child is unique, and if you have multiple children, each will have different tastes and interests. I have more than one, and each of them is different from their taste buds to their hobbies.

Many parents project their unfulfilled desires or regrets onto their children. For instance, parents who didn't do well during their school years might unconsciously set unrealistically high expectations for their children to compensate for their own perceived failures. Others feel pressured by societal norms, thinking, "Everyone is doing it, so I should, too." I was guilty of this. I used to enroll my daughter in various classes simply because "everyone is doing it." However, I eventually realized that this was straining our relationship, and I stopped those classes. We must remind ourselves that our children are not molds or shadows of our experiences.

Setting expectations for your child should involve a clear, consistent, and flexible approach. Establish long-term expectations but break them into manageable milestones. For example, attending university is a long-term expectation, but you should also set short-term goals along the way like maintaining good grades (based on your child's capability) and regularly completing homework assignments. These goals should be agreed upon with your child and be achievable by them. Celebrate their short-term achievements and allow them to savor success. This way, they learn that they can meet the expectations set for them. Review and adjust short-term goals as needed.

It's okay to set high expectations, but let your child know that falling slightly short of these expectations doesn't equate to failure. It's easy to get caught up in the pursuit of perfection, but we must learn to appreciate and applaud the progress made along the journey.

Compliment your child for their effort and accomplishments, as this reinforces the idea that the journey is also valuable.

Our children will then learn that they can surpass their expectations, that hard work pays off, and that they are loved unconditionally. Realistic expectations are about witnessing our children grow and helping them to develop in their unique ways.

Now, let's address unrealistic expectations from the perspective of parents because sometimes, even well-meaning parents unknowingly impose these burdens on their children. It's an instinct for parents to want the best for their children. There's nothing wrong with pushing your child to reach their highest potential, but there's a fine line between gentle encouragement and pushing too hard. Unrealistic expectations often stem from a place of love, but they can inadvertently create immense pressure and negatively impact your child's self-esteem.

In academics, your child might excel in storytelling, math, and languages or have a passion for learning new things when taught in the right manner. Hone these strengths and encourage them to excel in a way that aligns with their capabilities and interests. Avoid expecting rapid, profound changes from your child. Instead, inspire slow, consistent growth. Encourage them to progress steadily, as consistency is the key to long-term success. Remember, expecting a child who scored 50 percent on a test to suddenly achieve 75 percent is unrealistic. Focus on gradual and achievable growth and involve your child in the goal-setting process.

Not meeting expectations within a set timeframe is not a failure; it's an opportunity to learn and grow. Avoid pushing too hard, as sacrificing rest and leisure time can lead to burnout. You also need to be flexible in setting goals and expectations. Maintain balance in all aspects of life including work, fun, food, and personal development.

Guide your child to explore their interests and passions. Allow them to find what they are genuinely good at and set realistic, achievable goals that help them improve their skills. Imagine if you were learning a new language, dance form, or switching careers. You'd want to set reasonable, attainable goals for yourself, and children are no different in this regard.

Expectations aren't limited to our children: We also have expectations for ourselves. These self-expectations can be beneficial when they are realistic. They provide clarity, direction, and accountability in our lives, helping us strive toward our long-term goals. However, unrealistic self-expectations can lead to avoidance, confusion, and fear.

I talk to myself a lot; I call these conversations my personal pulse talks. Your internal dialogue plays can help you shape your self-expectations. Shift your mindset and rephrase detrimental thoughts. You can also keep a journal to track your thoughts and progress and write positive affirmations.

Don't rush to meet your expectations. You will have setbacks, and that's okay. Be flexible with your deadlines and remember that sacrificing your well-being for the sake of meeting expectations isn't realistic. Adapt your plans as needed. Rather than dwelling on your shortcomings, focus on what you've accomplished. This positive perspective will help you maintain realistic self-expectations.

Don't be so fixated on what you want to achieve. Take time to appreciate what you already have. Being present in the moment allows you to recognize the joys in your life and enhances your overall well-being. Others often have expectations of us that can add to the pressure we feel. These external expectations, whether from family, friends, or society, can impact our well-being. Know where these expectations come from and evaluate whether they are healthy.

If someone close to you has unrealistic expectations, understand their origins. People often adopt expectations from their families, society, or personal experiences. While understanding doesn't change your perspective, it can facilitate a meaningful discussion and potentially lead to an adjustment in expectations.

Healthy expectations in relationships can promote growth and understanding. Evaluate whether the expectations imposed on you are appropriate, fair, flexible, and fulfilling. Healthy expectations are accepting, respectful, honest, and productive, and they contribute positively to your well-being.

Embracing Mistakes as Learning Opportunities

The silver lining of any screw-up is the undeniable fact that mistakes are teaching moments. I learned so much more through becoming a parent than I did reading about parenting in books. Of course, learning has consisted of making mistakes and learning from them.

If parenting came with a manual, it would easily be the size of an encyclopedia. Like you, I've had my fair share of parenting blunders, and I've realized that they are more than just mistakes. They are real-life lessons.

I have more than one kid, and I quickly discovered that what works for one doesn't necessarily work for the other. Parenting has been a dance of one step forward and sometimes two steps back, riddled with mistakes. Over the years I've been a parent, I've learned volumes about what not to do.

One of the most valuable lessons you can teach your children is that it's okay to make mistakes because we're all human. You can't teach them to be perfect, but you can show them how to handle their mistakes, learn from them, and grow stronger. Resilience is a far more valuable trait than perfection. Many of us grew up in households where authority was unquestioned and apologies were rare. When you admit your mistakes and apologize to your children, you show them that you respect and value them as individuals. It doesn't undermine your authority; instead, it strengthens your connection and sets an example of humility and accountability.

You learn a better way when you fail. Failure is a part of life, and parenting mistakes teach you what doesn't work, helping you discover more effective approaches. For instance, when your attempts at family meetings turn into chaos, you can adjust your strategy. Over time, I have learned that weaving conversations into playtime before bedtime proved to be an organic and successful approach.

You can help your child understand the benefits of challenges and enhance their skills, both in execution and problem-solving. You can also help them build resilience and the ability to bounce back from setbacks. Encourage asking questions and asking for help when needed and teach them the value of self-assessment and self-regulation. You can also encourage them to reread information or directions and identify alternative strategies to approach the problem. Reinforcing the idea that learning from mistakes and misunderstandings is a valuable skill.

Coping With Parenting Challenges

Finding personal time for yourself as a parent can feel like a luxury, but you have to practice self-care if you want to be an effective parent. If you're struggling to carve out time for your interests and hobbies amidst your parenting responsibilities, it might be time to consider delegating some of your tasks.

One option is to hire a nanny or enroll your child in a daycare program. This can free up a portion of your schedule to pursue activities you've been longing to do.

Parenting a child with special needs comes with a unique set of challenges. In addition to the typical parenting issues, you face hurdles related to inadequate support, communication difficulties, and behavioral challenges. Early diagnosis of learning disabilities in children can make a significant difference in helping your child lead a fulfilling life and in assisting you as parents to better adapt to their needs.

When your child begins to ask questions about sensitive topics such as menstruation, sexuality, divorce, or death, it can be awkward to navigate these conversations. While you can't expect your child to understand what you are communicating, you can provide them with a foundational understanding that sets them on the right path. Don't shy away from discussing such topics with them. If you do, they will go ask in the wrong places and likely receive the wrong answers.

When discussing sensitive subjects with your children, try to use the right words. It might be tempting to substitute words you're uncomfortable with, but using the correct terminology helps your child become familiar with it. Additionally, try to explain these complex concepts in simpler, more age-appropriate language. This approach gives a quicker and more effective understanding, which ensures that your child feels supported and informed.

Children often test boundaries and challenge authority, which can lead to frustrating moments for parents. While the temptation to resort to threats or punishment might be strong, avoid this approach. When your child acts defiantly, be direct in your communication. Clearly state what you expect them to do, using a firm but controlled tone. For example, say, "I want you to pick up these toys and put them back in the toy box," rather than using vague questions like, "Will you put the toys back in the box?" This direct approach leaves no room for ambiguity and communicates your expectations.

Maintain consistency in your responses to disobedience, making it clear that "no" is not an acceptable answer. By addressing disobedience in this manner, you establish boundaries and reinforce your authority as a parent while promoting healthy communication.

Encouraging your children to eat healthy can sometimes turn into a battleground. You want them to consume vegetables and fruits, but you also want mealtime to be enjoyable without constant conflict. Involving your children in the process can be a successful strategy.

Teach your kids about nutrition, food labels, and the importance of making healthy choices. Create an environment where only healthy foods are readily available at home and allow them to make nutritious selections. You can also engage them in cooking or meal preparation, making it a fun and educational experience.

Be patient with your children's food preferences. Research suggests that it could take up to 15 attempts for a child to develop a liking for a new food. Additionally, consider occasional treats or special desserts when dining out to strike a balance between healthy eating and indulgence.

It's natural for children to test limits as they grow and gain independence. To effectively enforce rules and foster cooperation, periodically assess the rules you've set.

Ensure that your rules are reasonable and fair. When children understand that rules are in place to keep them safe and help them grow, they are more likely to willingly comply. Encourage your children to advocate for themselves and express their opinions within the framework of the rules.

For non-negotiable rules, establish clear consequences for disobedience in advance. The objective should be to teach rather than to punish. When rules are enforced consistently and fairly, they can effectively guide your children's behavior.

Dealing with children who lie can be emotionally draining, so try to differentiate between minor fibs and more significant lies. Make sure your children understand that they can confide in you and that honesty is valued in your family. Teach them about the consequences of not telling the truth, emphasizing the importance of trust, honor, and integrity.

Express your disappointment if your child lies but keep the lines of communication open. Encourage them to regain your trust and reassure them that they can always come to you with their concerns and confidence.

Establishing routines around important activities from an early age can help children view these activities as priorities. Create a dedicated time each evening for reading books before bedtime, even before your child starts school. As they grow, transitioning from reading to completing homework will become more seamless.

Ensure that your home environment is conducive to study time. Minimize distractions by turning off televisions and radios and designating a specific area for schoolwork. Keep in touch with your child's teachers to stay informed about their academic progress and needs.

Children naturally seek attention, so it's important to teach them how to do so appropriately. For instance, when toddlers start to show attention-seeking behaviors such as banging spoons or plates, respond with love and patience.

Encourage your children to verbally express their need for attention. Teach them to say, "Mommy, I need attention," and when they do, allocate a few minutes of undivided attention to them. This simple yet effective approach fosters healthy communication and helps children understand how to seek attention appropriately.

In an era of digital devices, managing screen time for children can be a concern for parents. You need to establish clear expectations regarding screen time. Set these boundaries before your child gets their first phone or electronic device, as it's easier to establish rules from the beginning. Communicate your expectations regarding screen time limits and usage. Consider creating a written agreement or contract that outlines the rules and consequences for breaking them.

Consistency is key when enforcing these rules. By doing so, you help your children develop healthy habits and maintain a balance between screen time and other activities.

Parenting often involves adapting and adjusting as your children grow and develop. Plans and expectations might need to evolve. As your children mature and become individuals with unique personalities and needs, be open to adjusting your parenting style accordingly. Flexibility and a willingness to allow change will help you navigate the various stages of your children's lives with positivity and resilience.

Nurturing Confidence Resilience in Your Child

Nurturing resilience in your child is one of the most valuable gifts you can offer. Resilience is like a life jacket your child can wear to swim through the often-turbulent waters of growing up. It allows them to bounce back from setbacks, adapt to change, and face challenges with confidence. Building resilience in your child is an ongoing process rooted in meeting their basic needs, fostering strong connections, practicing co-regulation, modeling resilience, maintaining a predictable rhythm, and allowing for downtime.

Imagine a car trying to run on an empty gas tank; it will sputter and stall. Similarly, when children are tired, hungry, or haven't had enough exercise, their emotional state can go haywire. Their little bodies and minds need a solid foundation to function optimally, and that begins with meeting their basic needs.

Children thrive on feeling connected and secure in their relationships, and this forms the cornerstone of resilience. As a parent, your role is to create a warm and supportive environment where your child feels cherished. When children have at least one stable and consistent attachment figure, they have a haven to return to in times of distress.

Attachment means more than just physical proximity; it's about being emotionally available to your child. They need to know that they can express themselves and be accepted by you. This deep connection not only nurtures resilience but also enhances their capacity to plan, monitor, and regulate their behavior, helping them to respond effectively to adversity.

At birth, a baby's nervous system is far from fully developed. This means that children rely on their caregivers to help them regulate their emotional and physiological states. This process is known as co-regulation, where parents provide the support and stability necessary for their children to find emotional balance.

When babies become stressed and dysregulated, they often can't self-regulate. Co-regulation is akin to teaching them how to ride a bike with training wheels. As parents, you initially hold the bike steady, gradually allowing them to become more independent. Similarly, you provide nurturing and soothing support, helping your child learn to self-soothe over time. Each child has a unique timeline for this development.

When co-regulating, strive to maintain a calm and present demeanor in the face of your child's distress. By doing so, you make it easier for them to find their way back to emotional equilibrium. This can involve comforting physical touch, gentle tones of voice, and allowing your child the time they need to become regulated.

Children are keen observers of their parents' actions. They learn by watching you navigate life's challenges. Therefore, one of the most effective ways to instill resilience in your child is by modeling it yourself. When you take a deep breath before losing your temper or cope with stress through self-care, you're demonstrating resilience in action.

Your children are more likely to internalize these behaviors when they see you handling adversity with grace and determination. Balancing your needs for nutrition, sleep, exercise, and downtime ensures that you can be the resilient role model your child needs.

Predictability and rhythmic routines provide children with a sense of security, which is crucial for building resilience. Life is less stressful when children can anticipate what comes next. Imagine life as a dance with a familiar and reassuring rhythm.

Children thrive when they live in "event time" rather than "clock time." In "event time," the duration of activities is determined by the experience, not by a timeframe. This flexible approach allows for spontaneity, taking one's time, and lower stress levels. By maintaining a predictable rhythm and embracing "event time" when possible, you help create a stable and nurturing environment that builds resilience in your child.

Even adults can become overwhelmed by too much activity, and children are no exception. Your child needs ample unstructured time to process their environment, explore their interests, and simply be with themselves. Think of it as giving their minds and hearts a chance to breathe and reset.

Downtime is like a pit stop during a race. It's where your child can refuel, recharge, and reflect on their experiences. Encourage your child to slow down, engage in quiet activities, and have moments of self-discovery. This unstructured time allows them to digest life's events at their own pace.

Practical Worksheet: Our Bond-Building Playbook

Let's turn bonding into an adventure. Use these tables to create memorable moments with your child while strengthening your special bond. Have fun, ask questions, and make lasting memories.

Activity 1: Quality Time	Activity 2: Storytelling Nights
Goal: Connect on a deeper level with your child.	Goal: Bring out creativity and imagination together.
Instructions: Choose a special day of the week for bonding. Write it on the calendar together! What activity or adventure does your child want to do during your special time together?	Instructions: Find a cozy spot with comfy pillows and blankets. Take turns telling stories. They can be about dragons, superheroes, or even your own exciting adventures! Draw illustrations to go with your stories.
Questions:	Questions:
- "What's your favorite thing to do together?"	- "What's the wildest story you can think of?"
- "What's one fun thing you'd like to try during our special time?"	- "Who are the characters in your story?"
- "What would make our time together even more special?"	- "What happens next in the adventure?"

Activity 3: Outdoor Explorer	Activity 4: Master Chefs
Goal: Discover the wonders of nature together.	Goal: Cook up delicious memories in the kitchen.

Instructions: Plan an outdoor adventure. Is it a nature hike, a picnic in the park, or a scavenger hunt? Explore, observe, and collect treasures from nature.	Instructions: Choose a recipe together, whether it's cookies, a pizza, or pancakes. Put on your aprons and chef hats! Who's the head chef, and who's the sous chef?
Questions:	**Questions:**
- "What's your favorite thing about being outdoors?"	- "What's your favorite meal we can make?"
- "Can you find three types of leaves?"	- "What ingredient would you add to make it even better?"
- "What animals did we spot on our adventure?"	- "How does our kitchen smell right now?"

Activity 5: Artsy Creations	**Activity 6: Family Game Night**
Goal: Unleash your inner artists	Goal: Have a blast while being a little competitive.
Instructions: Set up an art station with paper, paints, crayons, and glitter! Create your own masterpieces. You can even make funny portraits of each other.	Instructions: Pick a family game for the night — board games, card games, or charades. Who's the game champion in your family?
Questions:	**Questions:**
- "What's the craziest thing you want to paint today?"	- "Which game do you want to play tonight?"
- "Can you tell a story about your artwork?"	- "Who do you think will win?"

- "How colorful is our art station right now?"	- "What's the funniest game rule you know?"

Activity 7: Kindness Crusaders	Activity 8: Tech-Free Time
Goal: Spread kindness and warmth.	Goal: Disconnect to connect.
Instructions: Make a list of kind acts you can do together, like baking cookies for a neighbor or writing encouraging notes. Team up and make someone's day brighter!	Instructions: Declare tech-free hours. What fun activities can you do without screens? Explore new hobbies or just chat.
Questions:	Questions:
- "Who in our community could use some kindness right now?"	- "What's something fun we can do without screens?"
- "What's the most creative way we can show we care?"	- "What's your favorite part about our tech-free time?"
- "How did it feel to make someone smile today?"	- "How relaxed do we feel without screens around?"

Activity 9: Memory Journal	Activity 10: Passion Projects
Goal: Capture your favorite moments together.	Goal: Share your interests and passions.
Instructions: Create a memory journal. Decorate it with your child's drawings and notes. Write down your adventures, big or small.	Instructions: Introduce your child to your hobbies. Whether it's gardening, music, or cooking, let them explore with you. What sparks their curiosity?

Questions:	Questions:
- "What's the best adventure we've had so far?"	- "What hobby do you want to try with me?"
- "What's a special memory you want to keep forever?"	- "What's the coolest thing about my hobby?"
- "How colorful and unique is our memory journal?"	- "How excited are we to learn something new?"

Takeaway Six

- Children thrive on feeling connected and secure in their relationships, and this forms the cornerstone of resilience. As a parent, your role is to create a warm and supportive environment where your child feels cherished. When children have at least one stable, consistent attachment figure, it offers them a haven to return to in times of distress.

- When discussing sensitive subjects with your children, try to use the right words. It might be tempting to substitute words you're uncomfortable with but using the correct terminology helps your child become familiar with it. Additionally, try to explain these complex concepts in simpler, age-appropriate language. This approach gives a quicker and more effective understanding, which ensures that your child feels supported and informed.

- You learn a better way when you fail. Failure is a part of life, and parenting mistakes teach you what doesn't work, helping you discover more effective approaches. It's okay to set high expectations, but let your child know that falling slightly short doesn't equate to failure. It's easy to get caught up in the pursuit of perfection, but we must learn to appreciate and applaud the progress made along the journey. Compliment your child for their effort and accomplishments, as this reinforces the idea that the journey itself is valuable.

- We all have those days, but what matters to your child is that you do a good enough job. This doesn't mean that you condone abusive or neglectful behavior. Instead, it means that you are okay with the fact that you will have days when you feel like you're doing a lousy job, and that's okay. Parenting is not about being perfect. It's about being present and willing to learn and grow over time.

- Self-compassion is a skill I advise you to cultivate. We are often quicker to extend a hand of grace to others than we are to ourselves. Imagine how you would comfort and support a friend who's going through a tough time. Now, extend that same kindness and understanding to yourself. When you're feeling judgmental or disappointed with your parenting, remember that you're human, and humans make mistakes.

- Perfectionist parents often compare themselves to other parents. This habit can be damaging because it doesn't consider the unique circumstances and needs of their family. You just want to be validated by others and measure your success based on what you see other families do. Comparing yourself to others can fuel insecurity and undermine your confidence.

CHAPTER SEVEN

Strengthening the Parent-Child Bond

"That's what children are for — that their parents may not be bored."

— Ivan Turgenev

"Behold, children are a heritage from the Lord, The fruit of the womb is a reward."

— Psalms 127:3 (NKJV)

A study by the University of Minnesota found that children with strong parent-child bonds were more likely to have higher GPAs, better attendance, and fewer behavioral problems in school. They were also less likely to experience depression, anxiety, and other mental health problems (Egeland 2001).

Parents who spend more time with their children and engage in meaningful activities with them are more likely to have strong parent-child bonds. Another study by the University of California, Berkeley found that parents who spent at least 15 minutes per day in one-on-one time with their children were more likely to have strong parent-child bonds.

George MacDonald once said, "To be trusted is a greater compliment than being loved." I wholeheartedly agree. From the moment these children come into this world, they are drawing conclusions about the world and the people who are living life with them. Building a trusting relationship with your child is an ongoing commitment, but it forms the cornerstone to having a solid relationship with your child.

Building Trust and Connection

"Whoever is careless with the truth in small matters cannot be trusted with important matters." — Albert Einstein

This is where we all get it wrong. This quote strongly emphasizes the vital importance of honesty and integrity in a parent-child relationship. Let's take it piece by piece, shall we?

"*Whoever is careless with the truth in small matters...*" — This part of the quote suggests that if a person, in this case, a parent, is not trustworthy in the little things, it'd be very difficult to confide in them or discuss matters of great importance with them. The other part, "*Cannot be trusted with important matters*", implies that if a parent shows a lack of integrity or honesty in small, inconsequential things, it raises doubts about their reliability in more significant and crucial matters, particularly when it comes to parenting.

Trust is built over time through consistent honesty and integrity. If you are dishonest or careless with the truth in small matters or cannot act as a confidant, or more suitably, a diary, you can erode the child's trust in you. As a result, when important or serious issues arise, the child could seek guidance from other sources. In some cases, those sources can provide harmful solutions.

To build trust between you and your child, you must create an environment where your child is free with you and comfortable to express their thoughts, feelings, or actions. If this is lacking, your children might act in a deceptive or insincere manner, presenting different faces or personalities to different people or in different situations. They become deceptive and can start to hide their true thoughts, feelings, or intentions behind a façade.

Most traditional parents think that if they put their foot down, the kids will automatically respect them and do their bidding. That is not the case. It just creates fear in the child, making them think twice before talking to you about issues. If you demand compliance by force, they'll lie and learn how to play different cards. And when you find out the truth, you'll get angry, which causes you to make irrational decisions like getting excessively strict, thus straining the parent-child bond.

Research has shown that excessively strict parenting can have negative effects on a child's development and well-being. Children raised in overly strict households often experience higher levels of stress, anxiety, and depression. The constant pressure to meet strict standards and the fear of punishment can harm their mental health.

Overly strict parenting can sometimes lead to rebellious behavior in children. When they feel controlled, they might be more inclined to defy rules and authority, which can lead to conflicts. Strict parents often make decisions for their children without allowing them to learn from their mistakes. This can limit a child's ability to become independent and make sound choices as they grow older.

So, how do you begin building a trusting relationship in a family? And what do you do when trust is broken, and you need to regain trust between a parent and a child?

The first and most important is this: If you say that you will do something, DO IT. The most important step to building trust with your child is to follow through at all times. Sure, life happens, and there might be times you can't follow through. When this happens, be sure to address the "why" with your child. Don't break promises, and only make promises that can be kept. You might not be able to control certain situations, so consider that before uttering the words, "I promise" to your child. One broken promise is all it takes to lose your child's trust.

While your job is to teach respect, you also have a responsibility to show respect. This means you'll have to be an example of a respectful person to your child while still being the parent in charge. When a child grows up respected, they are more likely to confide in and trust their parents. We can still be the parent in charge while respecting our children, their accomplishments, and their needs.

It's important to maintain age-appropriate levels of honesty, but if you make it a point of duty to be constantly honest with your child, they will begin to trust you naturally. It's better to honestly answer a hundred questions from your child than to risk breaking that trust. Social media has bred an epidemic of public shaming of children. While our kids might need discipline, making a spectacle of it is inappropriate. In fact, such actions could destroy any trust you've built with your child. Discipline with discretion. Your child is watching everything you do, and their observations help them form their opinions of whether you are trustworthy. It's crucial that you model the behaviors you want your child to practice.

For instance, if you expect your child to make their bed every day, you should make your bed every day, too. If you expect your child to speak respectfully to others, you should do so as well. The more often your child sees you upholding the values and rules you teach, the more trusting they will be of you.

Lastly, nothing builds trust more than owning up to your errors. There isn't a perfect parent on this planet. We're bound to screw up, and that's okay. However, when you slip up, apologize to your child, and let them know how sorry you are.

Cultivating Empathy in Parenting

Empathy is the ability to understand and share the feelings, thoughts, and perspectives of another person. It involves recognizing and experiencing the emotions and experiences of someone else. Empathy in parenting, however, refers to the ability of a parent to understand and be in tune with their child's emotions, thoughts, and perspectives. It involves not only noticing what a child is feeling but also showing care and responsiveness to such feelings.

Empathy changes us as parents and changes our relationship with our children. When you can cognitively understand and tolerate your child's perspective, you are less likely to become inappropriately angry, aggressive, or respond poorly to your child. When you develop emotional empathy, it makes you well-attuned to your child's inner emotional world.

Empathy also significantly influences the parent-child attachment style. A parent who is in tune with their child's emotions develops a secure parent-child attachment, which is critical for the emotional and psychological health of our children. This is because a secure attachment concerns the protection, care, and security of the child.

When we feel empathy, we can see the world from another person's perspective. This can lead to a deeper understanding of their experience and a more compassionate response. A highly empathetic person is often in tune with non-verbal cues such as body language. They will notice the body language of the people around them and read it as a sign of their emotional state.

This can really help you connect with your child. At the core of empathy is the idea that you can put yourself in someone else's shoes and understand how they feel because you have felt that feeling yourself in the past.

People who have been through personal pain and suffering are often very good at this. They can know and understand other people's emotions because they have experiences with those emotions.

A particularly privileged person might have great sympathy for someone else but find it difficult to connect on an emotional level. They might have a hard time picturing themselves in a tough situation because they've lived a life where those situations have not arisen. As a parent, though, this level of empathy comes easily. When a teenager is having a disagreement, a term they often use is, "Put yourself in my shoes," expecting you to see the world from their perspective. A parent who lacks empathy can't do this, thereby putting a dent in the relationship with their child.

You might be that block in the neighborhood that loves to celebrate with others. You want the people around you to be happy. When they're joyful, you feel the same joy bubbling up within you.

Parenting is the ideal version of this feeling of empathy. When our child is happy, giggling, or feels a sense of accomplishment, the same feelings overwhelm us. Children learn empathy from watching us and from experiencing our empathy for them. It is vital to model empathetic behavior in your interactions with not only them but others. When we empathize with our children and show empathy, they develop trusting, secure attachments with us. Those attachments are key to their wanting to adopt our values and model our behavior, and therefore, to building their empathy for others.

They also learn empathy by watching those you acknowledge and appreciate. They'll notice if you treat a server in a restaurant or a mail carrier as if they're invisible. They'll notice if you welcome a new family at their school or express concern about a child in their class who is experiencing a challenge.

Practice active listening when your child speaks. Show genuine interest in their feelings and concerns and ask open-ended questions to encourage them to express themselves. Children are born with the capacity for empathy, but it needs to be nurtured throughout their lives. Learning empathy is, in certain respects, like learning a language or a sport. It requires practice and guidance. Regularly considering other people's perspectives and circumstances helps make empathy a natural reflex and, through trial and error, helps children get better at tuning into others' feelings and perspectives.

To help with this, you should ensure that when you're enforcing rules, you do so with lots of empathy and understanding. Explain why certain rules are in place and how they benefit everyone. By doing so, you not only cultivate empathy in your home, but you're also building a mutual understanding between you and your child while letting them know that you're still in charge.

Effective Listening and Validation

Regardless of your occupation or position in life, listening skills are paramount to effective communication. You might wonder what effective listening is and how it pertains to communication. To better explain, listening is one major communication component between people. To convey messages, people must engage in speaking and listening skills. This back-and-forth pattern results in a conversation. However, many people admit that their attention has failed them at one time or another while holding a conversation, which usually results in a host of problems, including misunderstandings and frustration.

Essentially, the concept is simple: If your child feels genuinely listened to, they also feel respected and that what they are saying matters, therefore establishing trust. This concept is the backbone of effective listening, which in turn maintains and builds relationships.

Effective listening is defined as when a person can attend to a speaker, process what the speaker is saying, and respond appropriately. It is not enough to hear what a person is saying. One must absorb the meaning, reflect, and respond accordingly.

Effective listening and validation go hand in hand. When you listen actively and validate someone's emotions, you create a safe environment for communication. It not only aids in building trust, but it also helps to strengthen relationships and make the other person feel heard and understood, even if you don't necessarily agree with them.

When it comes to parenting, active listening, and validation means understanding what your child or teen has to say and giving your full attention to them while also encouraging them to share their feelings and be open to communicating their emotions.

Through validation, you can teach your child that all feelings are okay and that you are comfortable with even the most uncomfortable feelings. Actively listening helps you understand your child's perspective and where they are coming from. It is also a way of gaining vital information about what is important to them. It has nothing to do with a decision being made, nor is it a way to get the other person to do something.

One pitfall we get into is the need to rescue our children and "make them better" by helping them to stop feeling "bad". We tend to put on our problem-solving hats. We can help our children by teaching coping skills, but it is important to remind ourselves and our children that we do not want to "fix" by getting rid of the feelings. Instead, we should validate that the feelings exist, and learn how to tolerate and manage them. A parent's validating response does not always mean that we believe the intensity of the child's feelings is justified, but rather that we understand and accept that how they feel is valid for them.

For example, you pick up your daughter from preschool. She is crying and tells you that her friend took her favorite toy and stuck out his tongue at her. You show her that you are actively listening when you say, "It seems like you are sad about your friend taking your favorite toy." Your daughter continues to cry and nods her head. She says that she thinks her friend will break the toy. You show her that you are still actively listening by saying, "It's okay to feel upset. You think he'll break the toy, don't you?" At this time, your daughter calms down a bit. You and your daughter continue to talk, and she learns that it is okay to be upset. She has begun to learn how to label and cope with her feelings by talking to someone.

To show that you are actively listening as a parent, maintain eye contact with your child. It shows that your attention is on them and their words and try to give verbal cues and exclamations wherever necessary. Use words like, "I see," "Wow," "Tell me more," or "Really," to encourage them to continue sharing their thoughts and feelings. However, make sure you don't sound sarcastic; it can be counterproductive.

Resist the urge to interrupt. Also, learn to use open body language and avoid crossing your arms or showing you are distracted. Summarize what they're saying and show that you've been actively listening. For example, "So, if I understand correctly, you're saying..." Throw out questions that encourage them to be more open about their thoughts or feelings regarding the issue. This shows that you're genuinely interested in the conversation. Allow your child to express themselves fully without hastening them. Give them time to gather their thoughts.

Follow all this while keeping in mind that active listening is more than just listening, it's about understanding and connecting on a deeper level. You're not only proving that you are a great listener but also that you value their time. When you listen actively to your kids, you develop trust and commitment that help you build strong relationships with them. When you are devoted to your children's stories or struggles, you make them feel heard and respected. Because of this, they become confident that they can rely on you.

Misunderstandings and lack of recognition are easily avoided when you are fully committed to the discussion. Hence, active listening can help eliminate and resolve conflicts. Imagine your child telling you how much he prefers custard to chocolate. They repeat it three times and you still reply with, "Sorry, what?" That not only causes frustration but it creates unnecessary misunderstandings. To avoid this, try the active listening examples listed above.

Conflict Resolution Strategies

Although it's one of the most valuable skills you can have, conflict management is something many individuals shy away from. Conflict is inherently uncomfortable for most of us, in both personal and professional contexts, but learning to effectively handle conflicts in a productive, healthy way is essential — especially in regard to parenting.

While conflict resolution is a skill best built through years of practice and experience, starting with some of the most common and effective conflict resolution strategies will give you a strong foundation to work from for years to come. It brings the two parties together to figure out a solution to a problem rather than pulling them apart. You can't expect to have a conflict-free home as long as you are raising a child. They tend to bring out the worst in you at times if you aren't well grounded in your emotions, and trying to fix it alone will only lead to more problems. Instead, you should aim to ensure that everyone has the skills to handle conflicts in a professional manner.

There are many forms of conflict linked to parenting, and not all are bad. What is most important is the approach. You are a model to your children, so if you remain calm and respectful while addressing disagreements, it helps your kids learn how to manage conflicts. Differences in parenting and the influence of other family members can cause parental conflict. Our childhood experiences mean we all have ideas about how to parent our children, and these aren't always the same. Children generally learn from the adults in their families how to behave and interact. Can you do anything differently to show your children how to manage disagreements positively? Sometimes, little things like changing how you respond to situations as parents can have a positive effect on your children's behavior.

Finances are a major cause of worry for lots of parents. The thought of how to pay the rent, settle other bills, and afford the basic family needs can lead to stress and conflict in the household. Sometimes, debt, overspending, job loss, buying a house, or perhaps a drop in working hours affect income. Also, living in a cramped apartment where your children are unable to have their own space can pose a big challenge, leading to stress and conflict.

One cause of argument between parents and children, especially teenagers, is curfew. It doesn't matter what time you set, when kids don't come home when they're supposed to, their parents get worried. A worried parent becomes a scolding parent. When the teen *does* come home, they get an earful and a stiff punishment. No one likes to work for free, but occasionally, teenagers see doing chores as working for free. Their parents are likely providing something tangible as payment that the teenager might not be acknowledging. You are providing food, clothing, shelter, use of a vehicle, etc. But when you are young and self-centered, that's not enough payment for taking out the trash and cleaning your room. Allowances might not meet the adolescent's expectations, just like grades might not meet parental expectations.

When you notice yourself getting heated, have a strategy ready. "You may need to pause and take some deep breaths, request a time out, or just take a moment to center yourself," Psychology Today blogger Sarah Epstein said. Having the self-awareness to recognize when you need a break to compose yourself so as not to make an argument or issue worse — and agreeing to come back to the issue and not ignore it — is crucial to averting disaster.

When somebody is upset, especially during conflict, they often don't feel heard or understood. Repeating their statements and explaining that you understand why they're upset can quickly show that you understand their perspective. By acknowledging their grievance in their language, you show that you're listening and taking their complaint seriously. Statements like, "Oh, when I made that joke about your job, you were very hurt," can quickly diffuse a situation. As Epstein says, "When a person feels understood, there's room to re-establish the sense of connection."

Listen to emotions, not words. Normal verbal communication hinges on words, but arguments aren't normal communication. Attorney and mediator Douglas Noll, who's taught conflict resolution in maximum security prisons and the Hall of Congress said that in arguments, words hold less meaning than feelings. "You de-escalate by ignoring the words, paying attention to the emotions and feelings, and reflecting them back," he added. First, acknowledge your emotions. If you feel angry, frustrated, and disrespected, say, "I feel angry, frustrated, and disrespected." Then put analytical reasoning aside. Noll said that attempts to fix things and solve problems during fights escalate the conflict. Your desire to problem-solve arises from your unconscious need to soothe your anxiety around the dispute. Resist the urge to fix things: The secret is to de-escalate the emotions and *then* problem-solve. You de-escalate by ignoring the words and paying attention to the emotions and feelings.

Aim to end fights, not win them: This is a reminder of what the real goalposts are. Fights start because people want things they're not getting — respect, personal space, or a clean kitchen. But they often don't end with people getting what they want. This is especially true with kids.

Don't acquiesce to their demands, as appeasement will blow up in your face later. But give your kids a reasonable amount of choice and control over the outcome. Allow them to propose a different solution that works for everyone. It doesn't mean you should always give in, and the solution should be something you are comfortable with as well.

In a multi-year study conducted in the 1970s, influential relationship psychology researcher John Gottman found that happy couples balanced positive and negative interactions during conflicts. Gottman believed that happy couples maintained a ratio of five positive interactions — like showing interest or affection for the other partner – for each negative, creating the 5:1 ratio that Gottman's acolytes hold as the gold standard for successful relationships.

No one is perfectly considerate of their partner 24 hours a day. But as long as the majority of your relationship's interactions are positive, your conflicts will be more gentle and easier to repair. The Gottman Institute recommends keeping a journal of positive and negative interactions to help couples understand their ratio. Carrie Krawiec, a marriage and family therapist at the Birmingham Maple Clinic in Troy, Mich., recommends couples keep the ratio in mind during conflicts.

Let's say your kid left their wet towels on the floor after their shower. Again. Your natural impulse is to confront them the moment you see the mess on the bathroom floor. But you picked the wrong moment. Your reasonable request for your kids to pick up after themselves erupts into a full-blown war.

Also, keep in mind that stressed-out people aren't receptive to resolving conflict. Clinical psychologist Lucy Russell suggests that one should not try to resolve an issue when someone's "stress cup" is full. "For example, when a child comes home from school, his nervous system is likely to be overloaded from all the academic, sensory, and social demands of the day." Let them relax and decompress. Then knock on their door and talk to them about being responsible with towels. Try to deal with a difficult issue when the cup is full and it will probably overflow, causing irritability, anger, or a total meltdown.

Not all fights are worth fighting. And some of those worthless fights drag on for days, creating a vicious cycle. You know that place where your argument is taking place? You're not going to be there anymore. Maybe you're still mad. Maybe nothing is resolved. Maybe your partner implores you to stay. But if the argument's playing on a never-ending loop, put some distance between yourself and the argument. Take a five-minute respite from whatever heated conversation you find yourself in. Go for a walk around the block and consider whether the issue is one that you truly need to address or if you can let it go.

The key is to accept and follow open, respectful communication and seek solutions that consider the interests and well-being of both parties involved.

Quality Time: Meaningful Activities with Kids

Case Study

From the moment she held her newborn son, Lucy knew they shared an unbreakable bond. She enjoyed her months of maternity leave as her bond with little Luke grew stronger.

But these days, Lucy feels like she only sees her son at breakfast and dinner. Luke and Daniel, her husband, were chatting excitedly about the match they watched that afternoon, and she couldn't relate. She wasn't a football fan and couldn't afford to go to a match, so who could blame her?

But as she looked at them, laughing and giving themselves high-fives over the table, she started reminiscing. She remembered when Luke took his first steps when he said his first words, and how he clutched her hands tightly on the first day at kindergarten. She missed those times and the bond they shared.

These days, he only wanted to spend time with his father. Something happened at school the other day, and he would only talk about it with his dad. She was jealous of the bond he shared with Daniel and didn't know how to connect with him again.

As the days go by, our to-do lists become fuller and other priorities seem to take precedence over quality family time. However, research has proven that children who spend more quality time with their families are less likely to participate in anti-social behaviors such as drug and alcohol use. Showing your children that you love and care for them helps to keep them mentally and emotionally strong.

There is nothing more precious than the time you spend with those little bundles of joy. Every parent desires to create meaningful and lasting connections with their children, but in today's fast-paced world, it can be difficult to find the time and energy. However, by making a conscious effort to prioritize quality time with your children, you'll strengthen your relationship with them and also positively impact their development and overall well-being.

When your kids get home from school, you should ask how their day was. Nine times out of 10, you'll get the run-of-the-mill, "It was good." But was it? Whether it's over dinner or when you're tucking them in for bed, take time to find out how their day *really* went. What was the most interesting thing they learned? Did they try something new at lunch? Who did they play with at recess? The key to these conversations is making them less of a routine and more of a launching pad for quality time, communicating about things that are important in your child's day-to-day routine.

Let's face it: Life moves more smoothly when routines and rituals are in place. They help us — and our children — know what to expect. But instead of using this time to hurry along the moments before bed, for example, use it to create quality time with your kids. Sing to your child during their bath, picking a favorite song or a new tune you both just heard. Make teeth-brushing a game. If your child is into space, for example, you can pretend they are destroying asteroids with each stroke. Read a story at bedtime. If your child is older, let them read to you. When you take time to share things that pique their interest, they feel heard, seen, and appreciated.

Anytime you have the opportunity to celebrate your kids, do it! We aren't just talking about when they get an "A" or perform exceptionally well at a sporting event. Have they stepped outside their comfort zone to try something new? Did they give their all and put lots of work and thought into a project? Celebrating their successes is a great opportunity for quality time and reinforces positive behaviors.

Another fun way to spend quality time with your kids is to introduce them to games and shows you grew up with. Many games involve strategy and math skills, which help make learning fun. Many old shows and movies still tell timeless tales and teach valuable lessons, and you and your kids will be amazed at how quickly time flies when you're having fun together.

Kids have got to eat, and even the pickiest eaters will be on board with the opportunity to help plan and/or make their meals and snacks. Not only does having autonomy over their choices pique their interest in concocting creations, but cooking and creating together is a real-time example of showing your children that their ideas and opinions matter.

Have a "yes day". Funny, right? When you have a "yes day", you agree to say yes to every request your kids have for an entire day. Before you start to furrow your brows and roll your eyes, saying yes for an entire day won't be the headache you anticipate. Saying "yes" gives a sense of control in your environment, and children often don't have a sense of control. So when you say yes, they get to be in charge and you can also take that time to teach them what it means to be in charge.

Reinforcing Positive Behaviors

Positive reinforcement is only one of many forms of discipline, but from the perspective of positive psychology, it might as well be the most important one as it focuses on amplifying what is already good in our children and in ourselves as their caretakers.

Children quickly learn how to behave when they receive positive, consistent guidance. This means giving praise and attention when you notice your child behaving well and using consequences when you need to guide them toward more positive behavior.

Positive reinforcement can be used to encourage behaviors we want to increase. It can also be used to reward your child for practicing new skills like tying shoes or loading a dishwasher and can encourage them to continue doing such. Research suggests that the ratio of 5 to 1 in positive to negative emotions contributes to happiness, a similar ratio of positive reinforcements to other forms of correcting behavior (like negative reinforcement or positive punishment) should also yield better results, and ultimately happier children and parents (Fredrickson 2005).

For many parents, the natural tendency to correct behavior problems was ingrained in their upbringing and is usually well-intentioned, but over-reliance on this approach deprives us of the many opportunities to notice what our children already do well.

Telling your child how their behavior affects you helps your child to see their feelings in yours. Starting your sentences with "I" gives your child the chance to see things from your perspective. It's best to talk about feelings when you're both calm. When your child is behaving well, give them positive feedback or praise. For example, "Wow, you're playing so nicely. I really like the way you're keeping all the blocks on the table." Praise makes positive behavior more likely and misbehavior less likely.

As your child gets older, you can give them more responsibility for their behavior. You can also give your child the chance to experience the natural consequences of that behavior. For example, if it's your child's responsibility to pack for a sleepover and they forget their favorite pillow, the natural consequence is that your child will have to manage without the pillow for the night. At other times, you might need to provide consequences for inappropriate or unacceptable behavior. For these times, make sure you've explained the consequences and that your child has agreed to them in advance.

You should always keep things light and fun at home. You can do this by using songs, humor, and games. For example, you can pretend to be the menacing tickle monster who needs the toys picked up off the floor. Humor at your child's expense won't help, though, because young children are easily hurt by parental "teasing". It's also best to avoid jokes when your child is misbehaving, as this can accidentally reinforce the behavior by giving it too much attention.

Practical Worksheet: Our Bond-Building Playbook

Bonding with your child is not as hard as you think! These simple but fun activities can help you get started.

Eat a Family Dinner Together

Eating dinner together is not just about filling our tummies; it's a special time for bonding. Share a meal, talk about your day, and enjoy some quality time. To keep track, fill in the below:

- Date: _____
- What did you have for dinner? _____
- Rate the meal on a scale of 1 to 5 (1 being not tasty, 5 being super yummy): _____

Snuggle During Bedtime

Bedtime snuggles are cozy, comforting hugs that bring you closer. It's a perfect way to end the day. Share stories, dreams, and precious moments in each other's arms.

- Date: _____
- Describe how you felt while snuggling: _____
- Did you share any dreams or stories? [ ] Yes [ ] No

Read a Story Together Before Bed

Reading a bedtime story is a timeless tradition that builds love for books and strengthens your bond.

- Date: _____
- Name of the bedtime story: _____
- What was your favorite part of the story? _____

Invite Them to Learn to Cook with You

Cooking together is a delightful way to bond while being creative in the kitchen. Share recipes, teach cooking techniques, and savor the tasty fruits of your labor. Cooking is not just about food; it's about making memories.

- Date: _____
- What dish did you cook together? _____
- Rate your cooking experience on a scale of 1 to 5 (1 being not fun, 5 being super fun): _____

Bonus Fun Question:

- If you could invent a new recipe together, what would it be? _____

Checklist:

For each activity completed, circle the number below:

- Activity 1
- Activity 2
- Activity 3
- Activity 4
- Activity 5
- Activity 6
- Activity 7

Family Fun Time:

- Choose one activity from the checklist that you want to do again next week: _____

Parent-Child Bonding Challenge:

- Can you come up with a new bonding activity that you'd like to try with your parent/child? Write it down here: _____

Remember to have fun and enjoy these bonding activities with your child! Check off completed activities and keep this playbook as a special memory of your time together.

Takeaway Seven

- Trust is built over time through consistent honesty and integrity. If you are dishonest or careless with the truth in small matters or cannot act as a confidant or more suitably, a diary, you can erode your child's trust.
- Children learn empathy both from watching us and from experiencing our empathy for them. When we empathize with our children, they develop trusting, secure attachments with us.
- Through validation, you can teach your child that all feelings are okay and acceptable and that you are comfortable with even the most uncomfortable feelings. Actively listening helps you understand your child's perspective and where they are coming from.
- There are many forms of conflict regarding parenting, and not all are bad. What is most important is how you approach conflict. You are a model for your children, so if you remain calm and respectful while addressing any disagreements, it helps your kid also learn how to manage conflicts.

CHAPTER EIGHT

Embracing a Peaceful, Happy Life

"Now may the Lord of peace Himself give you peace always in every way."

— 2 Thessalonians 3:16 (NKJV)

Let me start this last leg with a favorite poem by M. Jolynn Rawson-Hunt, entitled "True Joy":

I'll be happy once I've done this certain thing.

We all say this often, not realizing what it brings.

We look only to the future for our happiness,

Letting life slip through our fingers in its fullness.

Will we really feel complete when the task is done

or look back and see how we missed so much fun?

Self consumed so we can't see anything else,

hurting those we love as well as ourselves.

So many things around us to be grateful for.

When seeking for an answer, willingly open the door.

So often, others see what's in front of our face,

but we're too blind to look as we're snared in the race.

What is this life supposed to be about?

Is it money, fortune, fame, or a big house?

When speaking to a man on his dying bed,

None of these answers are what he said.

Family, love, laughter are what we should seek.

These are the precious things that keep life from being bleak.

That second to the last line got to me. "Family, love, and laughter are what we should seek." Often, we are under pressure to pursue many things, such as a career, stable finances, a social life, and more. It can be easy to get caught up in the hustle and bustle of everyday life and forget about what is important: peace and happiness.

These two things are the foundation of a fulfilling life. They are what give us strength, support, and joy. When you have strong relationships with your children, you can experience happiness and success.

This last chapter is dedicated to discussing how you can enjoy a peaceful and happy life with your family. It's been a rewarding journey, and I'm glad you made it this far. Let's get to work.

Reflecting on Your Parenting Journey

Case Study

Nicole stepped outside and took a deep breath of fresh air. She observed the morning sun as it painted the sky in hues of pink and gold as she sipped her coffee. For the first time in a long while, she was at peace.

As she watched her children playing happily in the yard, she took a moment to reflect on the simple joys of motherhood. As she watched them happily chasing butterflies and laughing with abandon, a warm feeling overwhelmed her.

And in that moment, surrounded by the beauty of nature and the laughter of her children, she felt a deep sense of gratitude. She was exactly where she was supposed to be at this moment.

The future might hold challenges or uncertainties. But now, there is family, peace, and happiness, and that's all that matters.

Raising a child is both demanding and rewarding. It's a job without a schedule, limited breaks, and certainly no instruction manual. While countless resources are available to help parents navigate their roles, sometimes we find ourselves in emotionally challenging situations that put our parenting skills to the test.

Positive parenting self-reflection involves acknowledging our emotions, reflecting upon them, and finding ways to manage them effectively to foster improved communication and relationships with our children. It also entails contemplating the values and aspirations we hold for ourselves, our children, and our relationships with them.

So, how can you begin practicing positive parenting self-reflection? Dedicate 5-10 minutes each day to jot down your thoughts and feelings. You can use journaling prompts or write freely about specific situations or your child's behavior. For example, if bedtime is a constant struggle, reflect on your mood before bedtime and how different approaches affect your child's response.

Be present in the moment. In the hustle of daily life, it's easy to brush off emotions. After those tough parenting moments, take a couple of minutes to record your thoughts and feelings about the situation. This immediacy helps you accurately recall your emotions, making it easier to work through them later.

While finding alone time can be challenging, it doesn't always mean solitude. It simply implies carving out time for self-reflection. Whether your child is napping, or you have a short stroller walk, use those moments to be present with your thoughts and feelings without distractions like podcasts or social media. Self-reflection can be a little strange, especially at the beginning. Here are some self-reflection questions to help you get started:

1. What values do I want my children to have as they grow up?
2. What type of parent do I want to be?
3. Which parenting style best aligns with my beliefs?

4. Am I taking care of my needs?
5. Are specific stressors affecting my parenting?
6. How well am I and my partner working together toward our desired parenting style?
7. What tools help me parent consistently?

In the age of social media, it's all too easy to fall into the comparison trap, especially as a parent, and that can really affect your self-reflection. I've been there myself, constantly questioning whether I was doing this whole parenting thing right. Social media often amplifies these feelings. I'd scroll through my friends' posts and feel a knot of insecurity forming in my stomach. Their lives seemed so put-together, full of exciting adventures and seemingly perfect parenting moments. It wasn't just a comparison of life stages; it was a comparison of parenting skills. Why did Janice's baby sleep through the night at six weeks when mine was still waking up? Why did Maria's baby seem to hit milestones so effortlessly?

My anxiety spiraled, and I felt like I was constantly falling short as a parent. However, over the years, I sought help for my anxiety, and my journey toward self-reflection and personal growth began.

Through my experiences, I've learned valuable lessons that I'd like to share with you, dear parents. What's best for your family might differ significantly from what works for your friends, and that's perfectly okay. The decisions you make for your family should always be based on the best interests of your loved ones. Don't make choices solely because they're trendy on social media. You're the one who has to live with those decisions day in and day out.

Remember that what you see on social media represents people's highlight reels. You're only seeing the parts of their lives they want to share. Behind those perfect photos and status updates, everyone faces challenges and struggles. Parenthood comes with various phases, and they all pass eventually. Just because your friend's child achieved a milestone earlier doesn't mean you've failed. My children didn't sleep through the night until age five, and that was fine. What mattered most was that they were happy and healthy.

Don't let comparisons on social media dim your light as a parent. What you see online is never the whole truth. Trust your instincts, and most importantly, be confident in your parenting abilities. Over time, as you learn to shrug off the comparisons, you'll find yourself reflecting on your life with a brighter perspective, making the parenting journey not just easier but more enjoyable.

Celebrating Progress and Successes

The concept of celebrating progress is not only exciting but also incredibly effective. When you regularly celebrate progress, you stay motivated even when your achievements seem small because every step forward is an accomplishment worth recognizing. Celebrating progress is a simple yet invaluable principle that applies to various aspects of life. Whether it's in parenting, personal development, or another area, as long as you're making progress, you're on the right path, and your motivation remains intact.

I discovered the connection between progress and motivation while in school. I had a clear goal in mind – to complete my degree. However, I made a common mistake: I believed that celebrating my achievements could only happen after I completed my degree. I thought I needed to wait until the ultimate goal was achieved to celebrate my progress. Fortunately, I soon realized that this approach didn't make sense. Life is a journey, and you need to enjoy the ride. This realization led me to the concept of "celebrating progress", which applies not just to academics but also to parenting and virtually any endeavor.

You need to celebrate every step of the journey, no matter how small the achievement might seem. For parents, this principle can have a profound impact, even when applied to studying or other personal goals. By sharing your experiences with your kids and emphasizing the importance of celebrating progress, you can inspire them and boost their motivation.

The key takeaway here is that some is better than none. Any progress, regardless of its size, is better than no progress. Let's take exercise as an example. Suppose you've committed to an exercise program to get fit. If you only have 15 minutes to spare, those 15 minutes are better than doing nothing. Even if you can only manage 10 minutes, it's still better than 5 minutes. The concept of "some is better than none" applies to various aspects of life, including parenting.

When it comes to parenting, you have most likely faced challenges when trying to get things done with your children around or getting them to cooperate without nagging. When you celebrate progress, you're essentially rewarding yourself for your hard work and recognizing even the smallest achievements in your parenting journey.

Regardless of your specific goal, breaking it into smaller milestones allows you to identify and celebrate each step you take toward your ultimate objective.

By applying this concept to your child's progress, you shift your focus from what they're *not* doing to recognizing and celebrating their improvements. Instead of dwelling on their shortcomings, you'll interact with them on a more positive and personal level, which can lead to more effective communication and a stronger bond.

So remember, as long as you're making progress, you're on the right path. Take a moment to appreciate your achievements, no matter how small, and reward yourself. Celebrate your progress as a parent, and you'll find that this practice not only motivates you but also strengthens your relationship with your children.

Maintaining Consistency in DBT Skills

Maintaining consistency in Dialectical Behavior Therapy (DBT) skills is like tending to a garden of emotional well-being. Just as you nurture plants with care, you must cultivate your DBT skills regularly to reap the rewards of emotional stability and improved relationships. Start by setting realistic goals. Imagine learning DBT skills as a series of stepping stones. Instead of trying to leap across the river in one jump, take one step at a time. Begin with achievable goals, focusing on a specific set of skills that are most relevant to your current needs. By breaking your journey into manageable pieces, you're more likely to maintain consistent progress.

Like brushing your teeth or having a morning cup of coffee, make DBT skills practice a part of your daily or weekly routine. Consistency often stems from habit, so designate a specific time for practicing these skills. It might be in the morning before work, during lunch breaks, or in the evening before bed. The key is to make it a regular part of your life.

Use reminders to stay on track. Set alarms, calendar notifications, or reminders on your phone or computer to prompt you to practice DBT skills regularly. These gentle nudges will help you remember and reinforce the importance of consistency.

Maintain a diary or journal to track your DBT skills practice. Document which skills you've used, when you used them, and the results you experienced. This diary acts as a valuable compass, helping you navigate your emotional landscape. It allows you to identify patterns and motivates you to continue your journey.

Periodically review the DBT skills you've learned. Over time, it's easy to forget certain skills or lose sight of their relevance. Regularly revisiting them reinforces your understanding and application. DBT emphasizes acceptance, not just of others but also of yourself and your current situation. Understand that setbacks and lapses in consistency are part of the process. Instead of being overly self-critical, practice self-compassion. Gently guide yourself back to your skills practice when you veer off course. Remember, it's about progress, not perfection.

If you find it challenging to maintain consistency on your own, consider seeking professional guidance from a trained DBT therapist. They can provide personalized strategies and support tailored to your unique needs. Acknowledge your efforts and give yourself credit for your consistency. Recognize that maintaining DBT skills is a significant accomplishment on its own. Self-validation boosts self-esteem and keeps your motivation alive.

Self-Care for Lasting Peace and Happiness

Finding inner peace and lasting happiness might sound like a dream, but it's something worth trying out for your overall well-being and contentment. As parents, it's essential to cultivate inner peace, not only for your sake but also to set a positive example for your children.

Inner peace leaves an indelible mark on your mental health that acts as a shield against stress, anxiety, and depression. With inner peace, you can effectively navigate life's challenges without being burdened by excessive stress and negativity. This mental resilience allows you to be more emotionally stable and better equipped to handle difficulties.

Moreover, inner peace enhances your ability to build healthy relationships. When you're at peace, you're less likely to engage in destructive behaviors like jealousy or anger. You become more capable of forming positive connections with those around you, fostering harmonious relationships within your family and beyond.

Additionally, cultivating inner peace contributes to increased self-esteem. It allows you to recognize and appreciate your self-worth, regardless of external validation or societal pressures. This self-assuredness empowers you to trust your abilities and decisions, freeing you from the weight of external expectations.

Furthermore, inner peace leads to greater life satisfaction. When you're at peace with yourself, you're more likely to find contentment in your daily experiences and appreciate the present moment. You don't constantly seek validation or chase future goals; instead, you find joy in the ordinary moments of life.

Consider the impact of your living environment on your inner peace. A cluttered, chaotic space can disrupt your serenity. Dedicate time to decluttering, cleaning, and organizing your home. Eliminate items that drain your energy and hinder your progress. A tidy living space fosters a sense of calm and peace.

Incorporate gratitude into your daily life. Practice gratitude through journaling, meditation, or simply by taking moments to appreciate what you have. Gratitude shifts your focus from scarcity to abundance, promoting feelings of contentment and inner peace. Whenever you feel agitated, turn to gratitude as a remedy for inner turmoil.

Be mindful of your self-talk. Replace self-criticism with self-compassion. Treat yourself as kindly as you would a good friend. Change your internal dialogue from negative and unkind to positive and loving. Seek validation from caring friends and family and shift your mental focus to your positive qualities.

Establish clear boundaries in your relationships. People-pleasing and a lack of defined boundaries can disrupt your peace. Take time to identify and enforce your boundaries, protecting your mental and emotional well-being. You'll find that those who care about you will adapt to your needs once you communicate with them.

Learn the art of letting go. Holding onto grudges and negative emotions only hinders your inner peace. Forgiveness is a powerful tool for cultivating tranquility. While it can be challenging, choosing to forgive and release these emotions is liberating and contributes to your emotional and physical health.

Discover your life's purpose and identify your values and principles to determine your life's purpose. This sense of direction and meaning fills your life with fulfillment and satisfaction. It aligns your path with your passions and principles, creating a settled, calm, and resolved inner state.

Prioritize your physical health. Regular exercise, a balanced diet, and adequate sleep contribute to overall well-being. When you care for your physical health, you feel good, think more clearly, and are motivated in all aspects of your life. Exercise also produces hormones that promote calmness and relaxation.

Learn to say no when necessary. Saying yes to things that don't align with your values or priorities can create unnecessary stress and resentment. Politely decline when something doesn't work for you and remember that you have the right to set boundaries and protect your peace.

Balancing Work and Family Life

Balancing work and family life is one of the most common sources of stress for working adults. In this productivity-driven society we live in, more and more people are finding it hard to adequately fulfill their roles both at home and at the workplace. The delicate art of achieving this balance is essential for your overall well-being and maintaining a healthy family dynamic. As a parent, I understand the demands and pressures that come with your professional and family roles. You need to take proactive steps to achieve balance, and I'd like to share some insights to help you.

The constant hustle and bustle of daily life can overwhelm your mind with stress hormones, making it difficult to transition between work and family responsibilities. Stress-relieving activities such as deep breathing, meditation, or taking a walk can help clear your mind and promote relaxation. When you are relaxed and content, you can approach work and family life with a refreshed perspective and a greater willingness to engage.

To truly achieve a balance between your work and family life, you must prioritize it. It's a conscious decision that requires thoughtful consideration. For instance, when making career choices or decisions related to family planning, consider how they align with your desire for balance. Choose a job that challenges you without overwhelming you, and carefully assess your family's needs to ensure responsible and manageable growth. Making wise choices in these areas can set a solid foundation for achieving and maintaining balance.

Incorporating flexibility into your work environment can significantly ease the challenges of balancing work and family. Consider discussing options for remote work or flexible hours with your employer. This can allow you to work from home or another remote location, ensuring that you don't compromise your precious family time. Studies have shown that flexible work arrangements can boost productivity and job satisfaction, contributing positively to your well-being.

Establishing a daily routine can also work wonders in maintaining balance. A consistent routine helps you manage your time efficiently, ensuring that both your work and family obligations receive adequate attention. For instance, if you're an early riser, consider completing some household or work-related tasks before your children wake up. This allows you to enjoy quality breakfast time with your kids before they head off to school. These routines foster a sense of stability and consistency in your family life.

Prioritizing your health should also be non-negotiable. Without good physical and mental health, achieving a work-life balance becomes increasingly challenging. Dedicate time to activities that promote well-being such as maintaining a healthy diet, engaging in regular exercise, and getting sufficient sleep. A healthy mind and body are essential for staying focused, productive at work, and emotionally available for your family.

Take breaks from technology to reconnect with your family. The constant bombardment of emails, notifications, and social media can fragment your attention and hinder meaningful interactions with your loved ones. Set aside specific intervals during the day to distance yourself from your devices and dedicate that time to your family. Studies have demonstrated that disconnecting from technology can improve awareness, strengthen human connections, enhance sleep patterns, and positively impact emotions.

Establishing clear boundaries between work and family life is paramount. Determine which actions are acceptable and unacceptable in both domains. Boundaries serve as a protective barrier, safeguarding your work from family distractions and vice versa. For instance, you can make a rule that prohibits the use of cell phones at the dinner table, ensuring an uninterrupted family mealtime. By respecting these boundaries, you can strike a harmonious balance between work and family life.

Understand that achieving a perfect balance might not always be feasible. Life is filled with unexpected challenges and emergencies that can disrupt your equilibrium. Family emergencies might require you to compromise on work, and important work commitments can occasionally encroach on family time. While it's natural to encounter periods of imbalance, the key is to make a conscious effort to restore equilibrium. Don't be discouraged by setbacks; instead, keep striving for balance and progress.

Building a Support System

There's an African proverb that says, "If you want to go fast, go alone. If you want to go far, go together." I cannot agree more. This adage perfectly encapsulates the need for support in parenting. You can definitely become stressed when balancing the demands of work, family, and life. Parents often express the sentiment that they don't receive the support they need. Creating a robust support system requires a combination of factors including programs, policies, and scaffolding established by organizations, communities, and parents.

When you receive support, you become healthier and more relaxed, enabling you to better care for your child. Your actions set an example for your child. Demonstrating your willingness to seek support encourages your child to do the same when needed. Seeking also support demonstrates that you value and need the people in your life. It fosters a sense of belonging and importance among your support network.

Effective support for parents involves understanding, appreciation, comfort, and readily available assistance. These elements form the foundation of meaningful relationships, whether personal or work-related. Feeling seen, heard, and understood, along with experiencing empathy and compassion, characterize positive connections.

Unconditional acceptance and the comfort of friends are vital components of parental support. They can be hard to find in a world often filled with criticism, dogma, and parental bias. Despite societal pressures, parenting and professional success are not mutually exclusive. Great parents can be great professionals, and vice versa.

As a parent seeking support, focus on building relationships with friends who can give you unconditional acceptance and a safe space for open conversation. Be clear about your needs — whether you need a listening ear or a shoulder to lean on — without necessarily being bombarded with solutions. Invest time and effort in these relationships that allow you to be vulnerable and accepted and consider joining support groups with shared interests. Small, intimate groups will give you a secure environment for discussing your specific challenges and concerns.

Another aspect of support is authenticity in relationships. When creating a supportive life as a working parent, prioritize relationships where you can be yourself. Authenticity entails honesty, trust, respect, and open communication. In authentic relationships, you can express your values and personality while respecting others' perspectives. Pursue connections that encourage genuine self-expression and invest time in building these relationships above others.

Satisfaction with friendships is a third dimension of support that impacts how parents perceive overall support. During times of change or reflection such as the recent global pandemic, people have re-evaluated their priorities, placing greater emphasis on family and community connections. Consequently, many individuals have become more selective about their friendships.

As you build and expand your support network, consider quality over quantity. Prioritize relationships with individuals who inspire you, share similar interests, and offer mutual enjoyment.

A robust family support system is a valuable asset comprising everyone with whom you share positive relationships built on encouragement, understanding, and unwavering presence through life's ups and downs. The adage "we teach people how to treat us" holds true when forming a family support system. Demonstrate the support you want by actively supporting those you love and trust. Cheer them on in their endeavors, offer help when needed, and be there for them in times of difficulty. A reciprocal relationship of support can blossom from your actions.

Building a support system from scratch can be extremely difficult, so start by developing your existing relationships. Identify people with whom you share a deep connection and mutual trust. These are the ones you can turn to for support. Initiate conversations about your desire to expand your support network, highlighting the positive impact they've had on your life. Encourage them to be part of your support system's growth.

Don't overlook the people you interact with regularly such as coworkers, neighbors, and parents of your children's friends. They can offer additional layers of support, whether through safe playdates for your children, parenting advice, or community engagement opportunities. They can become valuable components of your family's support system without adding extra commitments to your schedule.

Childcare providers and schools are integral to your child's life. They are essential components of your family support system, as they invest in your child's well-being. Establish open lines of communication with teachers, principals, and other parents. Participating in school-related activities and maintaining positive relationships with these stakeholders can also strengthen your support network.

Be discerning about the people you allow into your support system. Toxic individuals who consistently bring negativity should be avoided. It's acceptable to maintain cordiality without inviting them into your inner circle. When dealing with negative individuals in other environments, express your feelings calmly and consider distancing yourself physically to minimize their influence on your well-being.

You can benefit from different kinds of support, from assistance with daily tasks related to raising children to managing a household. It includes help with childcare, finances, emergencies, transportation, household chores, and shopping. Family, friends, neighbors, and other parents can offer practical support.

Emotional support focuses on your well-being as a person. It involves having someone to confide in, share concerns and joys, and simply enjoy each other's company. This support typically comes from family and friends who are willing to listen, offer advice without judgment, and respect your feelings and experiences. At times, you might need more formal support, particularly if you encounter persistent challenges or emotional distress. Don't hesitate to seek professional help from resources such as your General Practitioner (GP), whom you can consult for guidance on health, well-being, or referrals to appropriate services. Child and family health nurses can also give you advice and tips on child development, health, and parenting. Parent and family support organizations specialize in providing assistance, resources, and guidance to parents facing various challenges. You don't have to go through life alone with so many people around you, just reach out for help, and I am sure you will get it.

Practical Worksheet: My Ongoing Peace and Happiness Plan

My Current Situation

What things currently bring me peace and happiness?

_____
_____
_____
_____
_____

What things currently cause me stress and unhappiness?

_____
_____
_____
_____
_____

What are my goals for peace and happiness?

_____
_____
_____
_____

My Action Plan

For each of the things that cause me stress and unhappiness, what can I do to reduce or eliminate them?

_____

_____

_____

_____

For each of my goals for peace and happiness, what steps do I need to take to achieve them?

_____

_____

_____

_____

What are my timelines for achieving each step of my plan?

_____

_____

_____

_____

My Support System

Who are the people in my life who can support me in my journey to peace and happiness?

_____
_____
_____
_____
_____

How can I reach out to my support system for help?

_____
_____
_____
_____
_____

What resources are available to me to help me achieve my goals for peace and happiness?

_____
_____
_____
_____
_____

My Self-Care Plan

What do I need to do to take care of myself physically, emotionally, and mentally?

_____
_____
_____
_____

How can I schedule time for self-care in my busy life?

_____
_____
_____
_____

What are some specific self-care activities that I enjoy and that make me feel good?

_____
_____
_____
_____

My Ongoing Review

How often will I review my peace and happiness plan?

_____
_____
_____
_____
_____

What adjustments will I need to make to my plan as needed?

_____
_____
_____
_____
_____

How will I celebrate my successes along the way?

_____
_____
_____
_____
_____

Takeaway Eight

- Positive parenting self-reflection involves acknowledging our emotions, reflecting upon them, and finding ways to manage them effectively to foster improved communication and relationships with our children. It also entails contemplating the values and aspirations we hold for ourselves, our children, and our relationships with them.

- Celebrating progress is a simple yet invaluable principle that applies to various aspects of life. Whether it's in parenting, personal development, or another area, as long as you're making progress, you're on the right path, and your motivation remains intact.

- Just like brushing your teeth or having a morning cup of coffee, make DBT skills practice a part of your daily or weekly routine. Consistency often stems from habit, so designate a specific time for practicing these skills. It might be in the morning before work, during lunch breaks, or in the evening before bed. The key is to make it a regular part of your life.

- Inner peace leaves an indelible mark on your mental health that acts as a shield against stress, anxiety, and depression. With inner peace, you can effectively go through life's challenges without being burdened by excessive stress and negativity. This mental resilience allows you to be more emotionally stable and better equipped to handle difficulties.

- A robust family support system is a valuable asset, comprising everyone with whom you share positive relationships built on encouragement, understanding, and unwavering presence through life's ups and downs.

Thank You

Make a Difference with Your Review!

Dear Incredible Reader,

Bravo for completing our book! Your dedication to finishing this journey is truly inspiring, and we can't thank you enough for being a part of our story.

As you reflect on the adventure you've just completed, could you take a moment to share your experience? Your thoughts and reflections could light the path for readers who are just starting out.

Your honest review serves as a guiding light, showing the way for others to know what adventures lie ahead. It helps highlight the unforgettable moments, the lessons that stuck with you, and how this book has opened new doors for you.

Your review is a gift that can help others navigate their reading adventure.

Spending one or two minutes of your time to leave a review on Amazon can have a lasting impact on many moms and dads.

We're looking forward to hearing about your adventure! The links below are your gateway to sharing your valuable insights. Every word you share helps illuminate the way.

With heartfelt thanks,

Your Team at SpreadLife Publishing

📖 Leave a review on Amazon US 📖

📖 Leave a review on Amazon UK 📖

Conclusion

Unregulated emotions can significantly impact children's development and well-being. Modeling healthy emotional regulation, teaching them about emotions, and assisting them in developing coping mechanisms are crucial steps. DBT involves four key areas: mindfulness, distress tolerance, interpersonal effectiveness, and skills training. These elements will help you navigate whatever emotional challenges you have as a parent, and they will help your kids, too. Emotional triggers, those events or situations that spark strong emotions, were thoroughly discussed, and you'll discover how your emotional responses can significantly impact your mental and physical health and relationships.

Emotional intelligence is just as important as academic skills. It's the foundation for your child's personal and professional success. Encouraging them to face challenges builds resilience, and you equip them with essential life skills. Healthy coping mechanisms such as exercise, relaxation, and social support play a vital role in managing stress. Developing emotional regulation skills takes time and practice, and science-based strategies like reappraisal and self-soothing exercises can reduce emotional distress.

Children's emotional experiences evolve as they age, and different age groups require varying forms of support. Infants rely heavily on pre-wired emotional responses, while older children benefit from a more nuanced approach to emotional regulation. You have the unique opportunity to demonstrate healthy emotional regulation to your children. How you handle stress and stressors can serve as an example for them, teaching them valuable life lessons.

Successful self-regulation helps your child manage intense emotions, reducing feelings of shame and anxiety related to emotional struggles. Building a warm and supportive environment where your child feels cherished is necessary for their resilience. Open and honest communication is key, even when discussing sensitive subjects. Use the right words and explain complex concepts in simpler, age-appropriate language to ensure your child feels supported and informed.

Mistakes are part of parenting, and they provide lessons. It's okay not to be perfect; what matters is being present, willing to learn, and acknowledging that you're human. Extend the same kindness and understanding to yourself that you would offer to a friend facing a tough time. Avoid comparing yourself to other parents: Each family is unique, and your journey is yours alone.

Trust, honesty, and empathy form the foundation of a strong parent-child relationship. Building trust through consistency and empathy helps your child develop secure attachments. Conflict is a natural part of parenting, and it's essential to approach it calmly and respectfully. By doing so, you teach your child valuable conflict-resolution skills.

Self-reflection allows you to manage your emotions effectively, fostering improved communication and relationships with your children. You should celebrate success, no matter how small, as this keeps your motivation intact. Make practicing DBT skills a part of your daily or weekly routine. Consistency is key, and it helps you develop mental resilience, inner peace, and emotional stability.

You get to shape the lives of your kids: They are the clay, and you are the potter. You mold the lives of your children through your actions, reactions, and the way you handle emotions. It's a significant responsibility and a powerful opportunity. Can I say a word of prayer with you in closing?

Dear Heavenly Father,

As we conclude this book, we come before you with hearts full of gratitude for the precious gift of parenthood. We thank You for the privilege and responsibility of shaping the lives of our children, for they are truly a blessing from You.

Lord, we lift all parents and their children to Your loving care. We ask for Your guidance, wisdom, and strength as we navigate the path of parenthood. Help us to be patient and understanding, to model healthy emotional regulation, and to teach our children the importance of empathy and love.

We pray for the emotional well-being of our children that they may grow to be resilient, emotionally intelligent individuals. Grant them the ability to regulate their emotions, manage stress, and build strong, meaningful relationships.

Lord, we also ask for Your protection over our families. Keep our children safe from harm and guide them away from negative influences. Help us to create a warm and supportive environment where they feel cherished and secure.

May we always strive to be the best examples of Your love and grace. When we make mistakes, help us to learn from them and extend the same compassion to ourselves that You offer us. Let us always trust in Your plan for our families and have faith in Your unwavering love.

We thank You for the wisdom and guidance provided in this book. May it serve as a valuable resource for parents seeking to nurture their children's emotional well-being. Bless all families with Your love and peace, and may our homes be filled with Your presence.

We offer this prayer in the name of Your Son, Jesus Christ. Amen.

References

A. L. van Tilburg M, Edlynn E, Maddaloni M, van Kempen K, Díaz-González de Ferris M, Thomas J. High Levels of Stress Due to the SARS-CoV-2 Pandemic among Parents of Children with and without Chronic Conditions across the USA. Children. Published online October 21, 2020:193. doi:10.3390/children7100193.

Aldao, A. (2013). The future of emotion regulation research. Perspective on Psychological Science, 8(6), 575-594.

Child Mind Institute. (2023). Mindful parenting. Retrieved from https://childmind.org/article/mindful-parenting/.

Cognitive-behavioral therapy (CBT) for emotional regulation: A systematic review of the literature. (2019). Journal of Affective Disorders, 248, 231-245.

David and the Worry Beast: Helping Children Cope with Anxiety.

Davies, P. T., Sturge-Apple, M. L., Cicchetti, D., & Cummings, E. M. (2007). Exposure to marital conflict and children's emotional development: A meta-analysis. Psychological Bulletin, 133(3), 398-424. doi:10.1037/0033-2909.133.3.398.

Davis, M. M., Senghas, A., Brandt, F., & Ochsner, K. N. (2010). Neural correlates of cognitive reappraisal in extinction of conditioned fear.

Dialectical behavior therapy (DBT) for emotional dysregulation: A systematic review. (2017). Journal of Personality Disorders, 31(3), 288-312.

Egeland, B., & Sroufe, L. A. (2001). Attachment and early maladaptation: Developmental follow-up of a high-risk sample. Monographs of the Society for Research in Child Development, 66(1, Serial No. 265).

Emotion regulation and mental health. (2018). Annual Review of Clinical Psychology, 14, 155-181.

Emotional Intelligence: Why It Can Matter More Than IQ (1995) by Daniel Goleman.

Feeling Good: The New Mood Therapy (1989) by David D. Burns.

Gross, J. J. (2015). The handbook of emotion regulation (3rd ed.). New York: Guilford Press.

Gross, J. J., & John, O. P. (2003). Individual differences in two emotion regulation processes: Implications for affect, relationships, and well-being.

Heisel, M. J., & Cheavens, J. (2014). The self-soothing process: A review of the literature. Clinical Social Work Journal, 42(2), 130-140.

Identifying emotional triggers: A step-by-step guide. (2023). Healthline.

Managing emotional triggers. (2023). American Psychological Association.

Mind Over Mood: Change How You Feel by Changing the Way You Think (1995) by Dennis Greenberger and Christine A. Padesky.

Nakić Radoš S. Anxiety During Pregnancy and Postpartum: Course, Predictors and Comorbidity with Postpartum Depression. ACC. Published online 2018:39-51. doi:10.20471/acc.2018.57.01.05.

National Institutes of Health (NIH). (2022, June 29). Anxiety disorders. Retrieved from https://www.nimh.nih.gov/health/statistics/any-anxiety-disorder.

Ochsner, K. N., Silvers, J. A., & Buhle, J. T. (2012). Functional imaging studies of emotion regulation: A synthetic review and evolving model. Nature Reviews Neuroscience, 13(10), 664-677.

Shaw, D. S., Cummings, E. M., & Gillman, R. (2004). Anger and aggression in children and families. New York, NY: Guilford Press.

The Body Keeps the Score: Brain, Mind, and Body in the Healing of Trauma (2014) by Bessel van der Kolk.

The Highly Sensitive Person: How to Thrive When the World Overwhelms You (1996) by Elaine N. Aron.

The mindfulness solution: Everyday practices for everyday problems. (2011). Guilford Press.

The Science of Emotions: A Parent's Guide by Psychology Today.

The Science of Parenting by Margot Sunderland.

Translational Psychiatry: Yehuda, R., Flory, J. D., Bierer, J., Henn-Haase, C., Lehrner, A., Desarnaud, F., ... & McFarlane, A. C. (2012). Holocaust transgenerational effects on adult offspring mental health: A study of gene-environment interactions. Translational Psychiatry, 2(12), e173. doi:10.1038/tp.2012.122.

Trent, T. (2009). Scared of my own shadow: A memoir. New York: Scribner.

Troy, J. A., Shallcross, A. J., & Mauss, I. B. (2013). Emotional valence of distracted attention and cognitive reappraisal.

Waterford Institute. (2023). Mindfulness activities for parents. Retrieved from https://www.waterford.org/resources/mindfulness-activities-for-parents/.

Webb, T. L., Miles, E., & Sheeran, P. (2012). Developing and evaluating interventions to promote emotion regulation in children and adolescents. Psychological Bulletin, 138(1), 106.

World Health Organization (WHO). (2021, June 7). Mental health of adolescents. Retrieved from https://www.who.int/news-room/fact-sheets/detail/adolescent-mental-health.

Zero to Three. (2023). Mindfulness for parents. Retrieved from https://www.zerotothree.org/resource/mindfulness-for-parents/.

Printed in Great Britain
by Amazon